<small>ADVANCE PRAISE FOR</small>

Feedback Reimagined

"Positive feedback loops are crucial for creating virtuous cycles. Anyone interested in becoming better and bringing out the best in others, start here. *Feedback Reimagined* is a well-researched and practical guide for putting humans back into the equation for happiness and success."

—SHAWN ACHOR,
NYT bestselling author of *Big Potential* and *The Happiness Advantage*,
—MICHELLE GIELAN,
bestselling author of *Broadcasting Happiness*

"What the authors have accomplished here is incredibly profound while at the same time being simple and direct. Shifting away from peer criticism and lack of individual commitment, this approach teaches leaders and team members alike to hone their personal awareness, participate in the development of others, and collectively drive success as a team. I've seen nothing like it, and it is effective."

—SCOTT HOLSTINE, President at Teleflex

"I was a skeptic who respectfully argued that feedback should be anonymous. I was wrong. I've seen the difference in how people's eyes light up when they receive Shift Positive Method feedback. *Feedback Reimagined* is a brilliant catalyst to challenge your feedback ideas and to help people make long-lasting changes."

—SENIA MAYMIN, Chief People Officer and co-author of
the bestselling book *Profit from the Positive*

"Excellent! Engaging stakeholders has never been more critical in coaching for the client's success and increased trust for their team. The Shift Positive Method perfectly captures this by creating a social system of support and will leave you with the actionable steps to start implementing this today!"

—**Dr. Marshall Goldsmith,** Thinkers50 #1 Executive Coach and *NYT* bestselling author of *The Earned Life*, *Triggers*, and *What Got You Here Won't Get You There*

"What a refreshing method of feedback for leaders and teams today. *Feedback Reimagined* breaks down what makes feedback feel hard while paving the way for a different experience that's energizing and effective, reinforcing a culture of trust and psychological safety."

—**Mike Robbins,** author of *We're All in This Together*

"I had the pleasure of experiencing the Shift Positive Method while leading People, Talent and Culture at Wieden+Kennedy. The mindset shift is built upon principles I believe in, arranged in a manageable framework. As an HR executive, there are so many models to consider; this is one of the few that leads to culture adoption and change. I couldn't recommend it more to other CHROs or CPOs."

—**Keesha Jean-Baptiste,** Executive Level People, Talent and Culture Leader

"Once I was trained in the Shift Positive Method and learned the science and research behind what makes it so powerful, I made it the chosen method our coaches use with clients. I am thrilled that Pete and Jen have made Shift Positive even more accessible by writing *Feedback Reimagined*. Shift Positive is our go-to feedback tool for leaders wanting greater psychological safety, more engagement, enhanced collaboration, better performance, and stronger teams. I will be sharing this book with all of our HR partners!"

—**Ilene Schaffer,** MA, PCC, CEO and Executive Coach, Silicon Valley Change Executive Coaching

"When offering career advice over the years, I have often said, 'Know what you are good at, but more importantly, know what you are passionate about.' It was difficult for me to explain 'why' to people until I experienced the formal coaching around strengths-based feedback and took my team through the Shift Positive process. It's a breakthrough in getting alignment, positive energy, and motivation for yourself and your teams!"

—**Ty R. Silberhorn,** President & CEO, Apogee Enterprises

"My leadership strengths were crystalized and deepened with the Shift Positive Method. The process was a two-way mirror; it at once affirmed my self-awareness and offered insight into how others experience me. Armed with this profound knowledge, I see the possibility for my personal growth with greater clarity, optimism, and conviction to grow into my next leadership frontier."

—**Jenny Rao,** Head of School, Emma Willard School

Feedback Reimagined

Transform Your Organization
Through Positive Psychology
and Social Support

Peter Berridge | Jen Ostrich

modern wisdom
PRESS

modern wisdom
PRESS

Modern Wisdom Press
Boulder, Colorado, USA
www.modernwisdompress.com

Illustrations based on drawings by Peter Berridge
Cover design by Melinda Martin
Peter Berridge author photo courtesy of Audree Larson, Kliks Photography
Jen Ostrich author photo courtesy of Sarah Uftring

Published 2023

ISBN: 978-1-951692-29-2 (paperback)

DISCLAIMER

To my catalyst for change,
my post-traumatic growth compass, my inspiration:
Kathleen Grow Ostrich.
I hope you can see me now, Mom.

—Jen Ostrich

For Jenny, tu blave.

—Peter Berridge

Contents

Preface

I remember vividly when I first learned about the Shift Positive methodology. I had flown to Portland just a week after hearing from a dear colleague that the Shift Positive system of feedback was everything I had been searching for. I sat in a room with other coaches listening to the pure brilliance of the approach and felt like the negative feedback clouds had parted and the sun was shining, illuminating a new way of constructive feedback.

I had spent my 20-year career in corporate America and then as an executive coach watching the 360 process turn exceptional leaders into 5th graders. I witnessed leaders attach to the negative, anonymous comments and wonder who said what and why. It was derailing for my client and the coaching process. Sadly, traditional feedback approaches work against people's psychology instead of with it and are counterproductive to leadership and behavioral change.

When I learned about the Shift Positive methodology and the intelligence of each question in the process, I knew I had found something extraordinary for my clients. Not only was it an approach founded in research and evidence, but it was also an approach that helped people truly transform. As a CEO coach, I have had the opportunity to use the Shift Positive methodology across numerous Fortune 500 companies and see the incredible positive impact on leaders and the organization. I have watched clients in high-pressure positions flourish with this feedback system and build deeper relationships. I have seen decades of empty, confusing feedback turn into tangible behavioral change with this methodology.

I am grateful that this book shares the science and physiology of feedback, the tools to deliver it effectively, and the reasons constructive feedback is critical to building psychologically safe cultures. *Feedback Reimagined* illuminates how deeply important feedback is within an organization and how, when done right, we can create cultures of human thriving.

As a coach who has used this methodology for years, I am thrilled to see this book come to life, allowing everyone to imagine a new way to elevate people. This is the book we need to give to every coach, leader, and organization.

—Jamie Shapiro, CEO of Connected EC, PhD, ABD
Positive Organizational Psychology and author of *Brilliant:*
Be the Leader Who Shines Brightly Without Burning Out

Foreword

There are moments in life and your career when you experience something new that shifts your perspective forever. Doors open, and ideas swirl. A whole new way of thinking—*of being*—emerges. The content of *Feedback Reimagined* has been that for me, not just in my professional life but in my personal life as well; ask my kids. This book provides a revolutionary way of seeing how we can move people through successful development in a constructive and supportive way. This approach considers the whole person, intending to understand how that person lives and interacts with those around them. It empowers both the giver and the receiver of feedback to have interactive and constructive dialogue, build a better understanding of what is essential to success, see how that success can be achieved in partnership, and, most importantly, build allyship. I am grateful for Jen and Pete's work and the impact of their Shift Positive methodology on the business and coaching worlds.

My journey to the Shift Positive Method was paved by years of inadequate and disheartening feedback experiences for the individuals and businesses I supported. As a Human Resources practitioner and coach who's worked across billion-dollar industries from food manufacturing to medical devices and with individuals at all levels of the organization, I was desperate to provide feedback to leaders in a way that each person could hear, understand, and then be empowered by to take meaningful action. I was in a rut using the same bag of tricks wrapped in different packages. Inevitably, the feedback was rarely absorbed or taken as a "gift." A leader once told me, "*I know feedback is supposed to be a gift, but I would like to return this for an emotional refund.*" I remember this as the quintessential moment I felt utterly defeated as one of the people responsible for giving feedback in the company.

Those who have gone through traditional 360s have likely felt the same way. Often, the individual is left wondering who said what, what circumstances are being considered, and if everyone they encounter sees their deficits. The receiver of feedback usually glosses over identified strengths. They, in turn, fixate on the comments or numerical values that make them feel inadequate, resulting in an experience that is not as developmental or supportive as intended.

The Shift Positive Method changes the game. It offers support while creating a valuable impact for the individual and the people around them. When I began using the Shift Positive methodology in my work, I started providing in-depth, one-on-one interviews on behalf of the individuals on my leadership team. These interviews created an extensive report detailing individual areas of strength, articulating how these strengths have been used to create shared success. It then went further, naming the behaviors each person felt would make that leader more effective, which the leader could adopt immediately. The most unique aspect of the Shift Positive Method is that the feedback is **_not_** anonymous. This went against every traditional 360 report and tool I had used or been exposed to in my 20 years of working with teams and leaders. Though somewhat uncomfortable initially, this transparent way of providing feedback was fascinating. It later became evident that transparency is the secret sauce.

Throughout this book, the authors generously show how their method creates connection, alleviates fear, and provides strengths-focused feedback while naming new, more effective behaviors. Transparency and allyship allow for open dialogue about everything—both the good stuff and the tough stuff. The Shift Positive Method creates ownership of the message and openness to receive it. You'll learn in these pages why it is easier to develop new habits than to break negative behaviors.

A seismic shift occurred for me when I became the receiver of feedback in my own Shift Positive 360 report. I understood how I was viewed by my peers and teammates, what was working well, and how I could apply my strengths to improve outcomes and working relationships. I then had a clear picture of where I could adjust my approach. I also knew I could call on my allies to acknowledge and encourage my new behaviors.

Some of the most impactful conversations I have had in my career came from this process. Since the feedback came with the name of the person who gave it, I could go deeper with that individual. I better understood my impact on that person, both positively and, at times, not so positively. Simply put, it strengthened our two-way communication. The process enabled me to share the moments when I tend to withdraw and solicit ally support during those times. The Shift Positive Method helped our team see each other differently. We became allies in order to enable our shared success.

The lessons I have learned from the Shift Positive Method are innumerable and continue growing as I engage with colleagues, family, and friends. I have seen firsthand how this new way of feedback can be a gift worth giving and receiving. And I hope you do, too, as you embark upon the journey of *Feedback Reimagined*. If you're like me, you'll find yourself reaching for this wise approach to feedback again and again—in all facets of life.

—Lindsey Bauer, HR Business Leader,
Executive Coach & Developer of Human Potential

Introduction

We all share basic human drivers including *competence*—wanting to be good at what we do; *significance*—making a difference; *belonging*—being connected to others; and *autonomy*—having a sense of control over our lives. We see our goal as executive coaches as helping people achieve these innate drivers. When you see something that gets in the way of another's energy and purpose and ability to contribute, it's very disheartening. When you can create something that opens up the possibilities for meeting these basic human drivers, it is so rewarding and you want to share it. Feedback is one of those things. Done well, it can lead to growth and engagement. Done poorly, it can be devastating.

Our approach to feedback is intended to be about employee development—not evaluation. We've grounded our method in research and refined it through trial and continual feedback. The result—the Shift Positive® Method—helps to build trust, direct communication, two-way accountability, and social support. Through hundreds of coaching clients over the last eight years, it's been proven to create sustainable professional growth. We jokingly describe it as teaching dialogue skills disguised as feedback. We continue evolving our approach based on the experiences of those who use it, experience it, and share their insights.

There's a lot of information on feedback that we think is wrong. Certainly, not sharing feedback can be detrimental. There's also the idea that if you just tell people straight, they can take it. That being brutally honest is the best way to help others grow. But giving brutally honest feedback misses the mark. The feedback provider has a responsibility to see how their actions reinforce the actions of the other person. To see how their expectations are simply their own expectations, not truth. And when they go further to do the hard work of identifying what it is that they want rather than what they don't, they move from direct, brutally honest feedback to specific and constructive behavioral feedback.

We want to bring our method to HR leaders, learning and development professionals, and entire companies, so that leaders don't feel the frustration and hesitance of not knowing how to provide effective feedback to employees, and staff to each other. We want to take away the pain that the existing systems have created.

As executive coaches, we are also motivated to support other coaches. Conducting narrative 360 interviews is a common practice for coaches. However, coaches get stuck in an in-between place. They gather information from colleagues, summarize it, and then deliver it to the client. They become the courier of good and bad news. This is not a comfortable place to be. Yet, it doesn't have to be that way. Through our method, a coach can see their role in a new way. The role is not to gather information to provide to their client, but rather to work on behalf of the client to nudge the stakeholders (those peers, direct reports, managers, and others being interviewed) to become an ongoing system of support.

This creates much greater leverage for the client because they are no longer working with the coach in a vacuum. Instead, the client is engaging their whole people system to reinforce new behaviors as they happen. Clients are looking for this new approach. It's what companies are looking for to retain, develop, and grow their leaders of tomorrow. It's what today's workforce is wanting when they say, "Coach me; don't criticize me."

So, what led to us create this new way to address the challenges of traditional feedback? Our unique and multifaceted backgrounds have given us valuable insight into the importance of giving effective feedback. We understand its impact throughout an organization when it comes to employee engagement and growth, as well as the pain experienced because of feedback done poorly or insufficiently. Let us share more.

Pete grew up in the field of Human Resources, becoming Executive VP of Human Resources at a renowned health care organization serving people with disabilities. Among the HR functions was talent development, which included designing feedback systems—performance reviews, competency systems, talent planning, 9-box exercises, etc. Then, later, he was an executive coach, using 360-degree feedback tools. When offering feedback, he used to really plan out how to hold the conversation with people. He was one of the folks who said, "Feedback is a gift; you only get it a few times in your executive career." Or "This is confidential." "Don't give too much credence to one comment." Regardless, no matter how much good there was in the comments and results, the people would focus on what was wrong or the "opportunities." Pete recalls huge narrative reports from some of his client's 360 systems. Every time, the client would be concerned about who said what, distracted by trying to understand what it means, and left feeling like "I've already been working on this; maybe I can't change."

In 2010, Pete enrolled in the Master of Applied Positive Psychology (MAPP) program at the University of Pennsylvania, studying under the world's leading Positive Psychology researchers, such as Martin Seligman, Adam Grant, Angela Duckworth, David Cooperrider, and Ed Diener. Learning more about the concepts of strengths, Appreciative Inquiry, energy, motivation, social network analysis, negativity bias, and Human Systems was thought-provoking.

Through Positive Psychology concepts and research, he knew there would be applications to coaching and feedback. When he read in a meta-analysis that found that, alarmingly, more than one-third of feedback systems led to poorer performance and relationship breakdown, it really hit him. The intention of any HR leader and coach had always been to help people to grow and develop. This analysis, however, showed the results could be the exact opposite. So, what to do?

Pete studied and experimented. He looked at the basic assumptions and norms of feedback. He looked into solution-focused coaching and feedback methods and research. He networked with people steeped in solution-focused approaches. Then, he experimented by drafting new questions, digging into strengths, helping stakeholders reframe their perspective, and using the word "love" in interviews. He asked the stakeholders about themselves and their goals and dreams, focusing on the dynamics between the stakeholder and client. He asked them to imagine themselves in a better future and describe it. He asked the stakeholder how the client raised or zapped their energy.

Pete created a narrative 360, titled it the "Positive Approach 360," and began. And, it worked. People liked it. Pete started to get new clients from the people he had interviewed as stakeholders for other clients. At the close of the interview, the stakeholder would commonly ask, "How did she get one of these? How can I get one?" That was a huge aha—people actually wanted to get a 360. Kind of weird—it was like asking for a performance review! That's when Pete knew he had the start of something that could really change the feedback experience.

Cue Jen. Jen spent 14 years working in the advertising industry. From New York City to Philadelphia to Los Angeles, she spanned eight agencies, each with its own complex human system. During that time, she can recall only two experiences where a manager walked her through a written feedback report, both early on in her career. Not too long after that, Jen became a manager and ultimately a VP, the head of a department and responsible for her group's development. She remembers spending hours at night carefully writing what she hoped would be thoughtful yet helpful performance reviews. She was motivated to give them what she never had—specific examples, context, transparency on where comments were coming from, and optimism and support to reinforce that each of us can learn and grow.

Jen ultimately decided to change careers in 2012 to pursue entrepreneurship as a leadership coach. She had developed a strong interest in Positive Psychology after reading author and researcher Shawn Achor's work. Jen wanted to ensure any client that she worked with received the level of feedback they deserved. She was on the hunt for a 360 approach that felt different, yet effective. Jen's belief has always been you learn best through conversation, so she was interested in a narrative approach. In addition, when looking through a Positive Psychology lens, most survey-based 360s seemed harsh to her.

In 2013, Jen and Pete crossed paths at one of the annual Hudson Institute learning conferences for alumni. Pete was there to speak about Positive Psychology and coaching, and Jen was there to speak about building your brand as a coach. They met up for breakfast and shared their individual presentations, and that was the beginning of a friendship that was rooted in mutual respect and admiration for each other's strengths.

Jen saw Pete's deep expertise in the fields of Positive Psychology and Human Resources, and his ability to connect the two through simple application. Creating content—including both written and visual communication—and identifying smart ways to strategically position brands for growth are among Jen's greatest strengths, as Pete noticed. Recognizing their individual strengths and imagining the potential for collaboration led Pete to call Jen and ask, "Would you be interested in partnering up to share this 360 approach with coaches?" Jen paused for about five seconds and said, "Sure, let's do it." She immediately saw how to position this approach inside the "white space" of feedback, Positive Psychology, and corporations, and how to help others understand the inherent benefits of changing the way we experience feedback today. A partnership was born by the end of 2015.

Since then, hundreds of coaches have been certified in the Shift Positive 360°, and we love seeing them thrive as they bring the Shift Positive Method to their clients and companies. We enjoy seeing how this new approach to feedback makes them smile, brings relief, and launches them with fortitude to go out and use it with their clients. We love empowering learning and development professionals and HR leaders to rethink their entire collection of feedback and development tools to incorporate these concepts. And, we love seeing leadership teams prosper while modeling a new way of constructively engaging one another. This book is our way of sharing the method we've created to help organizations and employees overcome the inherent drawbacks of traditional feedback. Beyond being more effective, you'll see how the Shift Positive Method is actually energizing, helping you and your teams to truly grow and thrive. You will reimagine your feedback experience as you know it.

We have organized this book into three main parts. Part 1 sets the stage on feedback today. We'll cover the impact of ineffective feedback, discuss what makes feedback hard, and offer an invitation to see feedback in a new way. Then, part 2 dives into the details of the Shift Positive Method, explaining the core components and providing opportunities for you to reflect, practice, and apply in your situation. Finally, in part 3 we'll explore the future of feedback and what's possible when you build your entire company culture to align with the Shift Positive Method.

Throughout parts Two and Three, you will find some reflective prompts at the close of each chapter. We invite you to keep a companion notebook nearby where you can respond to the questions, practice the exercises, or journal your own thoughts on this approach to feedback.

If you fall into any of these roles, we know you'll find value in this book:

❖ A Human Resource Business Partner (HRBP) who's tried every approach to feedback and talent development with little success.

❖ A leader who's had a terrible or traumatizing feedback experience and wonders if there's a better way.

❖ A manager who can relate to seeing the problems of a peer or direct report but is not sure how to provide good feedback or is hesitant to provide feedback.

❖ A coach who's looking for a more effective way to bring feedback to light for their client.

❖ A CEO hoping to shift and strengthen their culture to meet the needs of today's workforce, driving more engagement and retention.

❖ An individual looking for a less intimidating, more human way to provide someone with constructive feedback.

We wrote this book because we care deeply about providing value—we truly want to make a difference in people's work lives and relationships. We believe that even one small shift can create seismic impact. So, as you read through the following chapters, we hope you'll identify one small shift you are willing to commit to in the spirit of creating more safe, energizing, and effective feedback experiences for all.

Let's dive in!

Feedback
Reimagined

PART ONE
The State of Feedback

In this section of the book, you'll see why feedback is hard and how most traditional feedback approaches are flawed from both a design and a delivery perspective. Chapter 1 is designed to help you understand and appreciate the landscape of feedback today from the various perspectives of the person giving it, the person receiving it, and even the HRBPs charged with implementing a feedback approach inside the organization. In Chapter 2, we'll teach you specifically why feedback feels hard, going through the research and science that illuminates the flaws in feedback today. By the end of chapter 2, we'll review a new approach to feedback, a way that feels safe and human and, as a result, is more effective.

CHAPTER 1

Feedback Today

Meg sits at her desk looking at the 3 p.m. meeting on her calendar that says "Joe's mid-year review" and feels dread. Her chest feels tight and she notices her heart beating a bit faster as the clock turns from 2:45 to 2:46. She actually feels queasy as she prepares herself for the meeting. She can't stop thinking about the last time Joe got feedback and how defensive he became, ultimately shutting down and walking out of his manager's office. Meg ponders to herself: *Why is feedback so hard? We have lots of ways to evaluate our employees and scheduled times of year to discuss how things are going, so why does it often feel traumatic for all of us involved?*

Meg has spent the last 15 years in HR and Talent Development and designed the feedback tools used in her organization. Now more than ever before, with several generations in the workplace and the newer generations expecting frequent, real-time feedback, Meg is questioning the way feedback is done. She finds herself longing for a new approach.

Joe's manager, Dave, is deflated by the experience with Joe as well, ever since feeling unclear about how to best support Joe's development journey. Six months ago, he came to Meg seeking support and guidance for how to help Joe to develop further. Joe is considered a high-potential employee yet has some key areas Dave would like to see him grow and strengthen before promoting him into a VP role. These areas include behaviors that fall more in the realm of emotional intelligence—being more self-aware of the amount of space he takes up, which often leads to his team not feeling seen/heard; his erratic emotional reactions when something goes wrong; and the perception that he's unwilling to hear or embrace others' perspectives.

As Dave imagines this mid-year meeting with Joe and Meg, he is feeling anxious about it. He's checked in with much of Joe's team; again, they report not seeing much difference from six months ago. They describe Joe as dominating, leading through his own perspective, and still having irregular emotional reactions that zap the team's energy. Dave isn't seeing how Joe is moving any closer to the path of VP, and this feels disheartening. Dave recognizes that Joe is a direct reflection of his own leadership and he's feeling a sense of loss. Dave is hoping Meg knows how to best handle this.

Joe looks at his watch while his marketing meeting comes to a close and sees 2:58 p.m. He realizes he's due in his mid-year review meeting with HR and his manager at 3:00 p.m. He immediately feels drained and weary. Joe thinks, *What are they going to say to me now? I wonder what my team said this time around and am I still on track for a promotion this year?*

Joe has tried his best these last few months to keep his cool when he gets frustrated, but it's not easy. He also remembers his manager Dave telling him to listen to other perspectives more, but often feels he's always needing to educate the team and help them understand his recommendation. He's unclear on what Dave even meant by that comment or where it came from. Nothing has been discussed since his annual review at the end of last year. All Joe knows is that he doesn't want to feel blindsided again. It's now 3 p.m., and Joe walks into the meeting feeling ready to defend himself—his armor is on and his palms are clenched and sweaty.

Can you relate to Meg, Dave, or Joe in this scenario? What comes up for you as you consider this 3 p.m. mid-year review meeting?

The Impact of Ineffective Feedback

This story is one of hundreds of experiences where a feedback approach has failed both the organization and the employee. In fact, when we look back through decades of coaching and HR experience, feedback—whether given ineffectively or not given at all—is among the biggest challenges for HRBPs, talent managers, leaders, and organizations overall. We hear over and over from leaders that they either haven't received clear, specific feedback in years, or the feedback they did receive left them feeling confused, triggered by negativity, and overall demotivated by not knowing who said what. They felt alone. Similarly, HRBPs say that they feel stuck because they know the current feedback systems aren't working the way that they need to, and that's a tough place to be when your role is to help others develop to be their most effective.

This is a common problem. While HR and talent managers design these approaches with the best of intentions, we have come to see how feedback today is not aligned with the way humans are hard-wired. As executive coaches and speakers, we've spoken to many audiences, asking them to share feeling words that describe their feedback experiences. The words that come up almost suggest a form of trauma—feelings such as: *unsafe*, *anxious, nervous, confused, alone, isolated, discouraged, deflated, frustrated, undervalued, worthless* . . . and the list goes on.

We've concluded that nearly every person we ask has had at least one terrible feedback experience, which as a result colors the anticipation and angst they feel for any future feedback conversation. Feedback doesn't feel safe. In turn, feedback conversations are not happening as frequently as they should or as effectively. Like Joe's experience, leaders are not developing professionally or personally, and as a result, engagement dips and attrition rises. This is a vicious cycle for you when your success is connected to how others succeed. It's a toxic cycle that you cannot afford to keep enabling. According to Recruiter. com, the turnover of the millennial generation alone costs the economy $30.5 billion annually.[1]

Feedback and Today's Workforce

Today's workforce, the majority made of up of the millennial generation, are saying, "Coach me; don't criticize me." The millennials and Gen Z grew up with the internet, where immediate response and instant gratification were normal, whether that was a "like" on social media or a Google search done in seconds.

> Today's workforce, the majority made of up of the millennial generation, are saying, "Coach me; don't criticize me."

This was reinforced when the trend of giving prizes out for any level of participation in childhood sports and activities began, controversially branding millennials as the "trophy generation." Despite this, the fact is that this generation is eager to see and understand what the path to success looks like. In a global survey that SuccessFactors conducted in 2014 in partnership with Oxford Economics, 1,400 millennials said they want more feedback from their managers. Further, they aren't looking for managerial direction, but rather more personal development—they simply want to know how to move ahead in their careers.[2]

Millennials are willing to do the work to get there, but too often their managers have not done the work to define what success looks like. Instead, managers are quick to point out lack of experience, weaknesses, or areas for improvement because it's likely that's how they were given feedback by their managers. What about a person's strengths? What is working? What could they do more of? How could they apply one of their strengths toward an area of growth? This is the feedback that will help someone to be more effective. This is what today's workforce is wanting, and rightfully so.

No matter what generation you belong to or where you are in your career, it's human nature to want to grow and contribute. When you aren't provided this clarity or opportunity, you are starved of a very basic need: to thrive. This is at the heart of our "why." As executive coaches, this became the essence of our mission: *to change the feedback experience one leader and organization at a time.*

No matter what generation you belong to or where you are in your career, it's human nature to want to grow and contribute.

Imagine having a feedback method for your organization that you can trust to deliver a safe, energizing, and effective experience each and every time. Imagine for yourself what it would be like to receive feedback on what people love most about you, what they think are your greatest strengths, what they truly appreciate about you. Second, imagine they go further to talk about what they think you *can do* to be even more effective. Next, imagine they go even further, committing to support you as you make those changes. Now, how does that feel?

In the next chapter, we'll show you what makes feedback so hard today, and then, how feedback can be more energizing *and* more effective. A culture where the entire system becomes invested in each other's development. But first, let's take a close look at what makes feedback hard and how feedback systems today are broken.

CHAPTER 2

Why Feedback Is Hard

Bring someone to mind that you work with. Think about feedback that you have for them. Really, don't hold back.

Now, could you say that to them? Perhaps not.

We'll explain why that is. However, first, what would it do for you if you could really share feedback openly and directly? If you could address issues in a way that felt constructive and was well received? How might it impact your relationships even outside of work?

What feeling did you experience when you read "Could you say that to them?" Was it fear, trepidation, dread, angst, anxiety, defensiveness, nervousness, or perhaps even a little queasiness? We often start our keynote presentation by asking (while holding up a beautiful gift box), "Would you like to receive a gift?" And then, "Now, what feeling just went through you?" We let people sit with that emotion as we watch smiles and nods in the group. Then, we ask, "Now, what if the gift . . . is feedback? Did the feeling change?"

That's what coaches tell their clients, and managers and HR leaders tell their staff. "Feedback is a gift. You only get it a few times in your career, so receive it openly and constructively!" However, that's just not how it feels.

Have you been in that place of receiving feedback, the gift? How did it feel to you? Maybe as coach or manager, you received feedback from colleagues to share with your client or employee, and you're in that in-between place. What is that experience like for you? When we ask these kinds of questions, nine out of ten times, the feeling words we hear back are negative.

We think we can handle the "tough stuff." Or that creating a culture of direct feedback will lead to better business results. Today, so much is written about radical transparency or radical candor. Often we even hear, "I want the critical feedback. I don't need the positive stuff." Yet research shows that even the word *feedback* is "often associated with evaluation"[3] and creates a reaction in the receiver. In later chapters we'll explain why these perspectives can come up short and leave out valuable elements of sustained change. But first, let's consider: What makes feedback hard? The answer is our psychology and physiology—specifically, we'll review SCARF, Mindset, and Negativity Bias.

SCARF

First, neuroscience. David Rock[4, 5] created the acronym SCARF, which was based on neuroscience research by Eisenberger and Lieberman[6, 7]. The research focused on how the brain responds to social threats. Using fMRI, they found the brain responds to social threats the same way it responds to physical threats. In fact, the same region of the brain lights up under social threats as it does with suffering or pain, going into fight or flight response when feeling threatened. SCARF stands for perceived threats to *Status*, *Certainty*, *Autonomy*, *Relatedness*, and *Fairness*.

Unexpected information in these categories causes our brain to react just as if we heard a startling noise behind us in a dark alley. So, while the information may seem logical or nonthreatening to the person providing it, the receiver's brain simply reacts.

> The brain responds to social threats the same way it responds to physical threats.

Let's say your manager comes into your office and announces, "Can I have a word with you? I'd like to make a couple of changes. We've been looking at scope of responsibility in the company and would really like to see you focus more. We'd like you to concentrate on new business. So, we're moving current clients under Ray and that will leave you with four of your eight direct reports and their staff to go after untapped opportunities. It'll mean a change of title, but your pay will stay the same. We'll figure out the title thing later. How does that sound?"

"How does that sound?" In your mind, "how does that sound?" sounds like you did something wrong, you screwed up, you can't handle current clients and new business, and you just got demoted. Also, who is "we" and why am I not part of "we"? That is our brain reacting to a change of *Status*.

Similarly, when we perceive a threat to *Certainty*—say a layoff is announced, or a medical issue comes up—the ground beneath our feet can feel unstable. We're unable to predict the future.

Autonomy is about having a sense of control in our life. When we have a micromanager, it feels like we've lost that influence over our little corner of the world. Just think about the last time you felt someone say or imply to you, "No, you can't do that." What did it feel like to you?

Relatedness is about connection and belonging. For example, your best friend resigns and is leaving the company for new opportunities. Your first thought might be: *Good for them. They're so talented.* Then your second thought is: *Hmm, maybe I should be looking too.* When we sense that loss of relationship, or feel different than others around us, we feel alone and our brain reacts.

Fairness is all about the perception of fair exchange between two people. When we perceive that we are being treated unfairly— perhaps we find out that our compensation is less than someone new to the company who has less experience—*ping!* Our brain lights up. This may not be logical, but it is what happens.

How many perceived threats can be triggered by feedback?

So, how many of these social threats (SCARF) can be triggered by feedback? All of them. It's a trick question. We may say that we want the truth; however, research has found that negative feedback not only creates a psychological threat but has physical consequences as well, including lethargy, anxiety, and depression. Research by Paul Green, Francesca Gino, and

Bradley Staats found that negative feedback results in recipients "shopping for confirmation" and seeking out people who will give more positive feedback.[8] Why? Because people generally need to know that they and the work they do are valued. These researchers said a common assumption is that what motivates people to improve is hearing the "brutal truth" and realizing that they're not as good as they think they are. However, they found that this just makes the recipient go find people who do not offer that negative feedback.

Mindset

Second, Mindset. Researcher Carol Dweck[9] focused on two theories of intelligence commonly held by individuals. One, intelligence is a fixed trait—a Fixed Mindset. Or, two, intelligence is malleable and can be increased through effort—a Growth Mindset. She found that a person's belief about intelligence impacts their effort, risk-taking, persistence, defensiveness, and ultimately achievement. People using a Fixed Mindset will choose low-challenge, low-risk opportunities and see failure as a reflection on them as a person. They perform lower when faced with tougher challenges.

People using a Growth Mindset will see high-challenge, high-risk opportunities and even failure as part of learning. Those individuals persevere and perform at a higher level.

So, what leads to a Fixed or Growth Mindset? Feedback. Providing person-oriented feedback and praise like "you're so smart" or "you're very good" actually reinforces a Fixed mindset. It's about "you." Conversely, providing effort-oriented praise and feedback such as "What was your strategy?" or "How did you prepare?" promotes a Growth Mindset. This leads to greater persistence, constructive solutions, creativity, and self-worth.

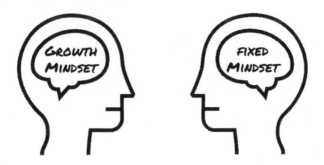

Why would someone who receives person-oriented feedback be less inclined to take risks? Perhaps because they don't want to lose the label—"the best," "the smartest," "highly promotable." Therefore, they take the safe route. So, how we offer encouragement or feedback is important, but it's not always easy. It can be easy to offer feedback that is person-oriented, while it takes more intention to offer behavioral or effort-based feedback. However, providing that effort or strategy-based feedback promotes a growth mindset and belief that change is possible.

Negativity Bias

The third concept that supports why feedback is hard: Negativity Bias. Negative emotions and perceived threats are experienced more intensely and grab our attention compared to positive emotions and events. This is an evolutionary adaptation—it is why we are still padding around on the earth. The emotion of fear causes us to take precautions, anger gets us to draw a line in the sand and make a stand, anxiety gets us to sock away seeds for the winter, etc. So, we are wired to see potential threats. A friend of ours, Dan Tomasulo, describes it this way: Cavemen Rog and Grog are standing outside a cave when they hear a noise inside. Rog says, "Hmmm, I'll go investigate." Grog says, "Nope, I'll stay here." We're decedents of Grog.

A couple of years ago on the University of Pennsylvania campus, Marty Seligman, one of the founders of Positive Psychology, talked about the negativity bias. The fun part was how Marty described the negativity bias. "The negativity bias is like the tongue," he said. "Our tongue swirls around our mouth ever vigilant to find a popcorn husk stuck in our teeth. When it does, full attention will be focused on that popcorn until it is dislodged. The tongue never just cruises around the mouth saying, oh, what beautiful, smooth teeth."

Well, feedback (even the word *feedback*) is the "husk," the potential threat. So, what happens when we get a "360" email asking our opinion about a colleague—their strengths and weaknesses? We instantly think of things that bug us that we'd rather they change. We quickly hit a six on a scale of one to ten, drop in a comment ("stop micromanaging"), and hit submit so we can grab lunch before the next meeting.

We can predict what happens next when our colleague opens the "confidential" results. They say, "Who said that?" Or, "If they knew how to do their job, I wouldn't have to do it for them!" Then, the colleague files the information under "C" for crappy co-worker and moves on with their day.

We are wired to see the potential threats (physical or social). So, we need to teach positivity to overcome our default response. To actually overcome our biology. With feedback, we're on the lookout for any sign of a potential threat or criticism. So, in 360s, performance reviews, and nine-box talent planning exercises, we tune into negative comments more than positive ones. If you've ever shared feedback with your coaching client or held a performance review with one of your staff, you know that you might share ten positive comments only to have the recipient tune into the one that could be perceived as negative.

Almost everyone has had a bad experience with feedback. In fact, many organizations are eliminating performance reviews because of this effect. An article by Wilkie asked, "Is the Annual Performance Review Dead?" and pointed out that GE, Accenture, Microsoft, Adobe, Gap, Medtronic, and some 10 percent of Fortune 500 companies have eliminated performance reviews or ranking systems altogether.[10] Further, the data on feedback systems isn't good. Meta-analyses from Nowack and Mashihi[11] and Kluger and DeNisi[12] found that more than a third of 360 feedback systems actually led to a decrease in performance and poorly designed 360 systems can increase disengagement, contribute to poor individual and team performance, and create discouragement and frustration.

More than 1/3 of feedback systems lead to a decrease in performance.

If you're an HR leader, executive coach, or learning and development professional, this is extremely disappointing and frustrating. We design and create feedback systems—performance reviews, 360s, compensation programs, talent planning systems, and promotional guidelines—because we want people to be their best at work. We want people to develop, grow, enjoy, and flourish— to increase engagement. Unfortunately, as noted above, these systems can often have the opposite effect. We created the Shift Positive Method because we believe these systems fail not because of poor intention, but because of design and delivery flaws.

Design Flaws

The first design flaw, we believe, is that feedback is often tied to decisions around compensation or promotion. The intent of this approach by Human Resources or a manager is to gather information in order to distribute a compensation pool or decide if someone is ready for promotion. However, intent is compromised as the feedback providers consider how their feedback will be received, who will see it, and what reflection it has on themselves, their own pay adjustment, or career aspirations.

Second, feedback, especially 360 reviews, are almost always confidential so they lack context and tone. If you're reading comments in a report, how do you know how they were intended or what circumstances are being described? Usually, you'll interpret those comments negatively. It's confusing. Coaches will report that the first thing their client tries to do is figure out who said what.

Third, generally, the focus is on what is not working, what is broken, weaknesses, or "opportunities." At least, that's how it feels due to the negativity bias. That leaves us wondering what we should be doing instead.

Finally, feedback systems lack ongoing support from stakeholders. Once it is given, it is rarely tracked, followed up on, or even noticed if the person works hard to make positive change. All of this leaves people feeling unclear, discouraged, isolated, and as though their colleagues are against them instead of with them.

Delivery Flaws

In addition to the design flaws with feedback, what's also broken is how feedback is delivered. We know about the relationship between feedback and employee engagement from Tom Rath's research in *StrengthsFinder 2.0*[13], which is captured in the chart below. In it, he describes a study of actively disengaged employees. Only one in 100 of the actively disengaged employees report that they received feedback on their strengths. Twenty-two in 100 reported that they received feedback on their weaknesses. What about the rest of the actively disengaged? Where do they come from? The largest portion of the actively disengaged reported that they didn't receive any feedback from their manager at all.

If a manager primarily...	The chances of the employee actively disengaging are
focuses on strength	1%
focuses on weaknesses	22%
ignores employee	40%

Tom Rath, *StrengthsFinder 2.0*

The idea that no news is good news is simply wrong. All too often, feedback isn't happening, and when it is, it's done poorly—focusing on what isn't working rather than strengths and what is working. So, the design and delivery flaws of feedback systems are working against us. However, in our experience, it doesn't have to be this way. We *can* change feedback to be the positive and constructive experience it was intended to be.

Looking at some basic elements of 360 feedback, we asked ourselves: Why are feedback systems confidential? Why do we have ratings and scales? Why do we talk about competencies rather than specific behaviors? Why do we have summary reports rather than individual, person- and context-specific feedback? Why do we ask about weaknesses or "opportunities"? We knew we needed to understand these answers to consider a more effective way and also to articulate to other seasoned executive coaches and HRBPs why a different approach is necessary.

When you consider these questions, it is apparent that many of these design flaws are in response to our biology and psychology: the negativity bias, SCARF, etc. People assume that these design elements are necessary. Feedback is often confidential because of the fear of retribution or, at least, hurt feelings. Competencies can be a way to consolidate information in order to create training programs. Scales are used to provide a sense of objectivity and measurement. Summary reports are a way for the coach to boil a lot of information down to bite-size pieces for the client.

However, as we'll describe, we challenge many of these assumptions. Further, we overcome a number of concerns through better design and delivery. We do this by defining what better feedback looks like and by incorporating the specific elements necessary to ensure a positive and constructive experience. Let's jump into what those elements include.

Psychological Safety and Trust

We know from Maslow's hierarchy that safety is a basic need for humans. How that comes into the workplace is worth considering, as research shows it's connected to not just effectiveness of teams but also employee retention. We can thank Harvard Business School professor Amy Edmondson for her definition of psychological safety: "a shared belief that the team is safe for interpersonal risk-taking." In turn, this creates a space where it is safe to speak up freely, to offer opinions or ideas, and of course to give and receive feedback.

In 2012, Google embarked on an initiative, named Project Aristotle, to study hundreds of Google's teams to figure out why some stumbled and others soared. The company's executives had long believed the best teams meant combining the best people, and other leaders believed the best teams were those who were friends outside of work. However, what the researchers found that really mattered was less about who is on the team and more about how the team worked together. The needs that employees communicated, in order of importance, were *psychological safety*, *dependability*, *structure and clarity*, *meaning*, and *impact*. Psychological safety was found to be by far the most important dynamic for effective teams. The researchers also found that individuals on teams with high psychological safety were less likely to leave Google and more likely to harness the power of diverse ideas from their teammates and bring in more revenue; they were rated as effective twice as often by executives.[14]

> The needs that employees communicated, in order of importance, were *psychological safety, dependability, structure and clarity, meaning,* and *impact.*

For psychological safety to flourish in a team, it is not enough for employees to feel respected by leaders. To feel comfortable taking risks, employees also need to believe that they can trust their leaders.[15] What Constantinos Coutifaris and Adam Grant reveal is the role vulnerability plays in establishing psychological safety, specifically with feedback. "Our research suggests that showing vulnerability—a topic that has attracted extensive interest in recent years (Brown 2015)— is an important avenue for building an environment in which employees feel comfortable raising concerns and suggestions."[16] When leaders were willing to share feedback they received in the past, it normalized vulnerability to the team and in turn increased the level of psychological safety the team felt.

Mayer, Davis, and Schoorman[17] developed a well-known model of trust in organizations composed of perceived ability, benevolence, and integrity. Put differently, when we perceive teammates as competent, as having our best interests at heart, and as ascribing to a set of values we endorse, we are more likely to trust them.

The reality is often that feedback says more about the person giving it than the person it is about. Our evaluations are deeply colored by our own understanding of what we're rating others on, our own sense of what "good" looks like for a particular competency, our harshness or leniency as raters, and our own inherent and unconscious biases.[18]

The ability to recognize this and take the opportunity to share the intent behind your feedback, to offer up some developmental perspective (versus being evaluative), can help to build trust. We really like the saying "With the right intent, you can share any content." When it comes to feedback, if the person receiving it truly trusts the intent of the person giving it, the stage is set for a safe and impactful conversation.

Feedback at Its Best

When you have a culture that promotes psychological safety, you can then build in more specific components to create the most effective feedback experience. Here are five specific aspects we see as essential to developmental feedback:

1. **Context:** The most helpful feedback gives specific examples, and it is also clear who is giving the feedback. Feedback offered by a manager versus that offered by a direct report is different and may require different solutions for change. Context matters.

2. **Strengths:** Each of us has talents that are natural and easier for us to leverage and create impact. When we are asking people to be their most effective, it's critical that they are clear and grounded by their core strengths. Those strengths also play an important role in the areas in which they need to grow.

3. **Solution-focused:** The feedback is focused on the solution or desired behavior instead of what's currently ineffective or seen as a weakness. The person is clear on what specifically *to do* differently (versus simply what to "stop doing").

4. **Timeliness:** Feedback is most impactful when it's in real time, within a few days of the moment occurring. This way both people can reflect on the situation and consider how it could have gone better or differently. Or, in the case of strengths-based feedback, it's easier for the recipient to recall what specifically they did in that moment that allowed them to show up leading with that strength. Frequency also matters. The 2018 Generational Kinetics Study[19] found that over 66 percent of Gen Z needs feedback from their supervisor at least every few weeks in order to stay at a job.

5. **Social Support:** There is a system of support around the feedback recipient. The provider of feedback is tasked with actively looking for progress and reinforcing it as they see it. Feedback shifts from being a one-way conversation to two-way accountability.

An Invitation to See Feedback in a New Way

Consider all of these elements making up a new and different way to experience feedback. Then imagine a workplace where managers regularly call out examples of strengths being leveraged and a culture where very few employees are disengaged. A place where it feels safe to have constructive, developmental conversations, where you trust the intention of the person sharing, and you're clear on who offered the feedback. A feedback culture that is centered around allyship—each employee actively supporting each other's growth goals. An organization that actively promotes a growth mindset. How does that sound?

We invite you to continue reading and see feedback through new eyes by learning each component of the Shift Positive® Method and how this approach can truly change the feedback experience for all. Over the next six chapters, we'll dive into a deeper explanation of the method, along with supporting research and real stories, to illustrate:

❖ How combining Positive Psychology and Human Systems into feedback can transform the experience to be energizing and effective.

❖ Why strengths-based feedback works and how to leverage strengths to be more effective.

❖ How to shift and articulate solution-focused feedback and move away from weakness/problem-focused behaviors.

❖ The importance of looking for the best of what is and envisioning an even more effective future through Appreciative Inquiry.

❖ How to build a system of social support to help drive successful, sustainable change.

❖ Why transparency is critical in feedback.

❖ The impact of a leader's energy on others.

❖ The role motivation plays in following through on feedback received.

You can create a feedback experience that studies what's right in people, reframes behavioral problems into solutions and desired outcomes, and creates a transparent yet safe two-way accountability between the leader and each colleague, leaving the leader energized by what's possible. This is the experience we are excited and grateful to share with you.

This is feedback reimagined. Welcome to the Shift Positive Method.

PART TWO

The Shift Positive Method

Are you feeling eager to understand how it's possible to change the feedback experience to be aligned with what we all intend it to be—a gift? We know we aren't the only ones with a fresh take on delivering effective feedback. However, our perspective is different in that it is based in science, research, experience, and refinement. As you learned in part 1, most feedback systems run counter to our psychology and physiology, creating unintended consequences. Now, in part 2, we will illustrate how, through the fields of Positive Psychology and Human Systems, we have carefully curated a method that supports what we need to be successful when it comes to growth and development.

In the next chapter, you'll see how to change the feedback experience through the two main anchors of the Shift Positive

Method: adopting a Positive Psychology mindset and creating systems of support. Then, in chapter 4, we'll explain the essential role that strengths play in feedback. Chapter 5 teaches you how to craft effective feedback that's still constructive by shifting from a problem-focused lens to a solution-focused one; this is the core of the Shift Positive Method. Chapter 6 explains why creating systems of support and leveraging allies are essential to growth and development. Chapter 7 illustrates how a leader's energy impacts the system. Finally, chapter 8 clarifies that even with effective feedback, illuminating an individual's motivation is the most critical component for sustainable change.

Throughout the rest of the book, there are some reflection prompts at the end of each chapter. We suggest that you have a place to take notes and apply some of what you're learning in real time, with actual people and scenarios in your day-to-day life.

CHAPTER 3

Changing the Feedback Experience

"I read my report before I go to bed or when I'm having a bad day because it makes me feel so good!" This is what Dee said to her coach after receiving her Shift Positive 360. This was two months after having a performance review that for the third year in a row focused on her "lack of executive presence," keeping her from being promoted to senior director. Yet, Dee was never given examples or a path to develop executive presence. She was simply told that until her manager and others felt she had it, she was not a candidate for promotion.

The VP of Talent Development, Karen, reached out to share this information with us to see if we were interested in taking Dee on as a coaching client. We could tell she too was feeling stuck in how else to help Dee. Karen described Dee as a highly valued employee and one in whom many saw potential. She also said Dee worked among a lot of loud and rather boisterous men and her style was quite different. When we spoke to Dee about this, she said after three years of the same feedback, the only thing she concluded was "I'm expected to act more like the men on the team," whom she saw as passionate, but also loud, rude (at times shouting or interrupting others on the team), and rather arrogant. This was not Dee. She was quieter yet thoughtful and perhaps a bit passive, especially in these group settings.

After meeting Dee and understanding things from her side as well as Karen's, we said she would take on the coaching assignment and felt we had just the approach to help both Dee and the system of people around her. The first thing we set out to do was get Dee the clarity and development path she so rightly deserved with a Shift Positive–certified coach and our 360. We still clearly recall how this one went. The coach interviewed eight of Dee's colleagues and learned so much about Dee, like how she was when she was at her best and what each person saw as her strengths. The coach heard that she was incredibly on point with understanding and reading her clients. She had a very strategic mind—able to connect dots and draw interesting insights. She was very thoughtful in the way she spoke and wrote. She was a fabulous manager and mentor to her direct reports, and that was evident in how they grew. She was creative and led with ideas for the creative teams to consider. These were all attributes the team felt were highly valuable. Dee's coach could see why the company chose to give Dee this opportunity to grow.

Then her coach started to hear how Dee was quiet, could be passive, and lacked the executive presence the firm was looking for. So, the coach brought each person back to the question at hand: How could Dee be even more effective? And can you help me understand what that would look like? Then the clarity began to surface. Many commented that Dee was very strategic and often had great contributions yet would surface them after the team meetings as opposed to during them. Her peers sensed she was more comfortable exploring her ideas/insights on her own to ensure they were right or perfect before sharing them. The theme became how she could be more transparent in her thinking, share her early insight or idea, and work through it as a team. If she felt more comfortable, one teammate offered, "I'd do a pre-meeting with her to kick around her thoughts and get her warmed up to sharing them in the larger group." Another encouraged her to capture her thoughts in short bullet points and have those ready to refer to in the large meeting. At the end of the day, the lack of executive presence really came down to showing up with more openness, collaboration, and transparency with the team. In essence, Dee's team encouraged her to share her strong strategic thinking sooner, in whatever way was most authentic to her.

True to the Shift Positive Method, each person also offered up a specific thing they could do to support Dee in her success. As mentioned earlier, one offered up a pre-meeting huddle. Another agreed to solicit her thinking in the meeting if she hadn't spoken up by the halfway point. Another offered to do more "drivebys"—stopping by her office spontaneously to just ask what was on her mind. This was all in an effort to help set Dee up for success by helping her to be more transparent and collaborative with her strategic thoughts.

When it came time to debrief Dee on her feedback report, she simply couldn't believe it. First and foremost, she had never heard her peers or manager call out so many things about her strengths—she had no idea how valued she was for her strategic thinking. Further, for years she had been hearing about a lack of executive presence and had her own assumptions about what that meant. Now, she was so beyond inspired, not just by the suggestions that were clear, but also by the offering of support from her colleagues to help her build these new habits. It wasn't going to be easy for Dee to shift from trying to ensure an idea was right to sharing openly when it wasn't fully baked, but she understood that's what the team believed would make her even more effective. And more importantly, that was the expectation needed to build the perception that she was indeed ready to be a senior director.

When it came time to review Dee's Shift Positive development plan with her manager, Karen (the VP of Talent Development) decided to sit in as well. She was very hopeful Dee would gain the clarity that the prior three years of performance reviews did not provide. When the meeting concluded, Karen told Dee's coach this was the first feedback approach she'd seen that helped leaders feel clear, energized, and supported in their development goals while also having a positive impact on those around them. It's true: The entire system of people who were interviewed felt more energized, clearer on Dee's value, and eager to put to work the commitments they offered up. No wonder Dee later said to her coach that she read her report after a bad day or before a big meeting—she simply had never felt so seen for who she is, clear on how to grow, and motivated to do so.

This was the first feedback approach she'd seen that helped leaders feel clear, energized, and supported in their development goals while also having a positive impact on those around them.

The Shift Positive Method

The Shift Positive Method is a unique combination that's grounded in the scientific study of Positive Psychology and the research behind Human Systems and creating systems of support. It's an approach that leverages strengths-based feedback, uses appreciative questions to understand the best of what is, takes a solution-focused approach to identify desired behaviors, utilizes system thinking to garner allies from the person's people system, and looks at the role that motivation plays in behavioral change. At its core, the Shift Positive Method brings Positive Psychology into feedback while creating a people system of allies around the person to aid in their growth and development.

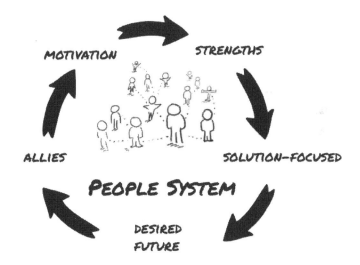

Overall, the model illustrated here is not just about the individual receiving the feedback; it is about creating an environment that is conducive to the person's progress and engagement, thereby creating fertile soil for successful growth. It is about creating deeper, lasting change, faster and with more dialogue, disclosure, and depth of thought by all participants—all allies in each other's success.

Let's take a look at the two main anchors of this method so you can begin to see how it truly revolutionizes the way in which people experience feedback.

One: Positive Psychology

Dr. Martin E. P. Seligman is founder of the University of Pennsylvania Master of Applied Positive Psychology program and director of the university's Positive Psychology Center. He was president of the American Psychological Association in 1998, during which his presidential initiative was the promotion of Positive Psychology as a field of scientific study. By simple definition, Positive Psychology is the scientific study of what is right with individuals, organizations, and communities—the study of well-being and flourishing. In short, what helps a person to thrive.

Marcus Buckingham quotes Dr. Seligman's 1998 inauguration speech for the American Psychological Association: "Psychology is half baked, we've baked the part about mental illness, disease, and damage, but the other side, things like strengths, what makes life worth living is unbaked. [Seligman] famously quoted there are 40,000 studies on depression and less than 400 on joy."[20] This mindset suggests that by studying the bad, we'll learn about the good. However, mental health is more than the absence of mental illness. Well-being is more than relief of suffering. Studying pathology, distress, and dysfunction is not the same as studying resilience, strengths, and growth.

Studying pathology, distress, and dysfunction is not the same as studying resilience, strengths, and growth.

Positive Psychology has blossomed with the scientific study of topics like resilience, strengths, relationships, optimism, hope, self-efficacy, Appreciative Inquiry, post-traumatic growth, mindset, habits, self-regulation, emotional intelligence, positive emotions, physical well-being, decision making, goal setting, compassion, mindfulness, and many more. Bringing Positive Psychology into the workplace is an invitation to see people through a different lens. To challenge yourself to look for what's right before trying to name or understand what's wrong. This goes against our basic biology, as we explained in chapter 2 with the negativity bias. However, it is possible to create that shift within yourself. Think of it as building up your own positivity muscle. Just like at the gym, it takes practice, intention, and repetition. Problem-solving is a tremendous skill, one that most of us hone on a regular basis and of which we can be proud. In addition, we can develop our skill of understanding what *is* working, what leads to this success, and how to achieve it more frequently. We can strengthen our skill of growing the positive.

When it comes to feedback, the Shift Positive Method applies several Positive Psychology findings and concepts that you'll learn about throughout the following chapters. The first couple concepts we'll introduce illustrate why Positive Psychology belongs in feedback.

The Role of Positive Emotions

Barb Fredrickson developed the Broaden & Build Theory, which helps us to understand the impact of positive emotions.[21] Her studies have shown that positive emotions lead to improved visual processing, creativity, resilience, performance, trust, memory for details, and better negotiation and decision-making.[22] In general, we perform better under the influence of positive emotions. That said, negative emotions do serve important functions, e.g., warning us of danger. However, we have discussed that as humans, we all have a *negativity bias*; i.e., negative emotions are stronger than positive emotions—they have a stickiness factor where we'll hold onto the negative ones longer. Conversely, we have a *positivity offset*—in general, we feel positive emotions more frequently than negative emotions.

 Through experiencing more positive emotions, we can broaden our thought-action repertoires for responding to situations and building our psychological and social resources. As it relates to feedback, this becomes incredibly important to balance out what can make feedback feel so difficult. As discussed in chapter 2, we know that we experience negative feedback with a fight or flight reaction ,as if we've experienced a physical threat (SCARF). However, when we are primed to feel positive emotions first, we are more open and better able to respond, rather than react.

Positive Affect

Positive affect is simply the experience of positive emotions, sensations, and sentiments. The frequency of positive affect most strongly predicts overall satisfaction.[23] This indicates that companies can increase employee satisfaction—and engagement—by focusing effort to promote a greater positivity ratio. A company can benefit by increasing small, frequent positive experiences. We love the example Shawn Achor shares in his book *Before Happiness*, in which he cites a secret ingredient that the Ritz-Carlton hotel utilized called the 10/5 Way. If a guest walked by a Ritz employee within 10 feet, the employee would make eye contact and smile. If that guest walked by within 5 feet, the employee would say, "Hello." Achor took this idea to a hospital system that was looking to improve performance, patient experience, and comfort. They trained thousands of employees in the 10/5 Way, and over time, the new behavior became contagious and changed the shared reality of the hospital.[24] Smiles are contagious, and the littlest bit of effort can increase positive affect.

Therefore, a company can implement positive interventions that increase positivity, and thereby increase engagement and performance. We saw this in the case of Dee and her experience with the Shift Positive 360. Not only did feeling seen for her strengths prime her positive emotions, it also allowed her to more clearly see how she could show up more effectively and address the feedback about having more executive presence. This increased her engagement level immediately, and ultimately her performance, as she pursued her development goals.

Growth Mindset

We learned in chapter 2 about Carol Dweck's work on mindset and how a person's beliefs about intelligence impact their effort, risk-taking, persistence, defensiveness, and ultimately achievement. To promote a growth mindset, her work shows that process/effort/strategy praise can have a positive effect, increasing persistence, encouraging constructive solutions and creativity, and promoting self-worth.[25], [26] As leaders, coaches, and HR leaders, offering encouragement or feedback is important; providing feedback specifically on employees' effort and strategies promotes a growth mindset and the belief that change is possible. This is the belief we want others to have when they receive feedback; as a result, it's another essential aspect of the Shift Positive Method.

In the Shift Positive 360 interview, several of the questions are framed to promote more of a growth mindset. This includes digging deeper for specifics around effort, strategy, and strengths, and highlighting when a leader is at their best or working effectively with another colleague. When coaches become certified in the Shift Positive 360, we teach growth mindset to ensure they are promoting this throughout the 360 interview and during the client debrief session when the leader receives the feedback. Finally, it's a core concept in our training for managers, what we call Shift Positive Applied. Leaders have their own "aha" moment in which they consider where they may be modeling a growth (or at times fixed) mindset, and we help them identify small shifts they can make to both model and build capacity in others for holding a growth mindset.

Two: Human Systems and Building Social Support

The second main anchor of the Shift Positive Method is building systems of support. From a systems thinking[27] perspective, we don't change by ourselves. We all live and work within a human system, and this system influences our behaviors. Take the classic example of the New Year's resolution. While it varies based on the source, we've seen dates as early as January 19 and as late as February 1 for the average time when people abandon their resolution. However, the people who garner a support system—get an accountability buddy to drive to the gym with each morning or have others with whom they commit to the goal—are more likely to stay committed to their goal for far longer.

A study done by Goldsmith and Morgan[28] looked at year-long leadership development programs across eight different industries and eight different organizations, taken from their client roster. The core components of the leadership development programs included receiving 360 feedback and reviewing with an external coach, identifying one to three areas for development, discussing those areas with colleagues, asking colleagues for suggestions on how to increase effectiveness, following up with colleagues to get ideas for change, and finally having colleagues complete a mini-survey 15 months after the start of the program.

One variable consistently emerged as central to the achievement of positive long-term change: the participants' ongoing interaction and follow-up with colleagues. Leaders who discussed their own improvement priorities with their co-workers, and then regularly followed up with these co-workers, showed striking improvement. Leaders who did not have ongoing dialogue with colleagues showed improvement that barely exceeded random chance.

> One variable consistently emerged as central to the achievement of positive long-term change: the participants' ongoing interaction and follow-up with colleagues.

What Goldsmith and Morgan concluded is not just that leadership is indeed a contact sport, but also that the key to developmental change is "learning to learn" from those around us and modifying behaviors based on their suggestions.

In the Shift Positive Method, we refer to the folks around the leader as their "people system of allies," and we promote the concept of allyship—being an advocate to drive change by engaging in each other's growth and development. In our 360 interviews, our goal is to learn about these allies—their backgrounds, what they're trying to achieve in their roles, what they see as future success. In the workplace, we often know our own roles or job description; however, we don't always know or appreciate what others are trying to achieve and why we're important to their success. In the Shift Positive 360, we ensure that's clear so both the leader (recipient of feedback) and their ally (interviewee) understand why this developmental feedback matters.

It can be very difficult for a leader to change unless the system recognizes and supports the leader's new behaviors. Just like the New Year's resolution, it's easy to fall out of a new habit with little to no accountability or support. It can be equally challenging for the leader when they do start to change, only to go back to a system that has not changed. We'll discuss more in chapter 9 about scaling and building a culture where the entire system, employees at every level of the organization, are working together to be allies in each other's growth. That is truly when we see not just one leader but an entire system thriving.

Your Role in the Shift Positive Method

Whether you are in talent development, an executive coach, a manager, or among the C-Suite, it is critical to understand your role and how it's different with the Shift Positive Method. Your role isn't to simply gather feedback or information on behalf of the leader. Instead, it's to be a *catalyst* for change inside their people system. Your role is to challenge participants to see through a new lens—help them to understand the power of Positive Psychology and what happens when we build people up through their strengths while also imagining them at their most effective and naming those desired behaviors. Further, it's to bring participants on board to become allies, to be willing to actively look for and reinforce the positive progress and growth they witness, to understand that this will ensure the person stays on track with ongoing progress toward their development goals. In being this catalyst for change and advocating for allyship, you are driving one of the essential, fundamental shifts of this method—taking feedback from a one-way conversation to two-way accountability.

To create the most impact with the Shift Positive Method, you must shift. This means shifting to a growth mindset where you deeply believe improvement and change is possible. It means seeing people with new eyes, noticing first what their strengths are and what is currently working well. It means shifting from problem-focused to solution-focused feedback, identifying clearly what better looks like or what a person can do to be even more effective. It is shifting to transparency and moving away from anonymous or confidential feedback. It is understanding that feedback is relational and always relative to the person who is providing it, not objective or inherently factual. Finally, it is realizing that people do not change by themselves and instead working to create two-way accountability, with each person becoming an ally in the leader's development.

How Shift Positive Is Different

The chart below gives a direct comparison of how the Shift Positive Method is different from traditional feedback. Consider how you have given and received feedback. What shifts will need to be made for you to adopt the Shift Positive Method?

Traditional Feedback	Shift Positive Method
strengths + weaknesses details ineffectiveness do less of	strengths focus builds on success do more of
lacks context problem-focused	specific context & behaviors solution-focused desired future
one-way feedback anonymous + confidential lacks follow-through	two-way accountability open + transparent allyship

At the end of each chapter, we prompt you to reflect on your insights and shifts as you consider feedback in this new way. Often, we find that the most seasoned professionals have the most "unlearning" to do to transition to the Shift Positive approach to feedback.

Chapter 3 Recap

❖ The Shift Positive Method combines concepts from Positive Psychology—what helps individuals and organizations to thrive—with research behind Human Systems and creating systems of support.

❖ We bring positive emotions into the feedback experience to capitalize on Fredrickson's Broaden & Build Theory. When someone is under the influence of positive emotions, they have improved visual processing, creativity, resilience, performance, trust, and memory for details, as well as better negotiation and decision-making skills.

❖ The frequency of positive affect most strongly predicts overall satisfaction. This indicates that companies can increase employee satisfaction and engagement by focusing effort on promoting a greater positivity ratio.

❖ Providing feedback specifically on the employee's effort and strategies promotes a growth mindset and a belief that change is possible; this is the belief we want others to have when they receive feedback.

❖ We don't change by ourselves. It's essential to be an advocate to drive change by engaging in each other's growth and development as allies, thereby shifting feedback from a one-way conversation to two-way accountability.

❖ Your role isn't to simply gather feedback or information on behalf of the person; it's instead to be a *catalyst* for change inside their people system. Therefore, you must have your own shift in beliefs to successfully implement the Shift Positive Method.

Reflection Prompts

Here is your first opportunity to reflect on what you've learned so far. (You'll find a section like this after each of the remaining chapters.) Our goal is to help you apply what we're sharing to yourself, your team, and your world and see what impact it has for you. We suggest capturing your answers in a notebook or on your laptop, and as you read further, you'll have more opportunities to apply what you're learning in real time.

1. What stands out about Dee's feedback experience at the start of this chapter?

2. How could a Positive Psychology approach create a positive shift in your workplace?

3. What do you notice about yourself when under the influence of positive emotions?

4. As you look back to childhood and throughout your professional journey, do you relate more to a fixed mindset or a growth mindset?

5. How can you play a more significant support role to anyone for whom you provide feedback?

CHAPTER 4

Strengths: The Essential Role of Strengths-Based Feedback

When you hear the word "strength," what comes to mind? When you consider strengths as a part of feedback, what comes to mind? Is it the same? Different?

What we've found is strengths are often seen as things you are good at. Conversely, if you have a weakness, that is something you're bad at. We have also seen how people confuse the notion of positive feedback with strengths-based feedback, which is something entirely different. So, let's unpack this. Here we'll dive into your strengths, why they matter, the role they play in feedback, and how they can help you improve areas of growth.

What Is a Strength?

Instead of thinking about a strength as something you're good at, we like Marcus Buckingham's definition: "A strength is an activity that strengthens you. It draws you in, it makes time fly by while you're doing it, and it makes you feel strong."[29] You are your most engaged and energized when you are using your strengths. The application of strengths is what allows a person to reach that optimal balance between skill and challenge, defined as finding flow by psychologist Mihály Csíkszentmihályi.

"A strength is an activity that strengthens you."

This combination of energy and engagement is also what makes strengths unique to you. Again, you can be good at something, but that doesn't mean it's a strength if it's not something you enjoy or are energized by. For example, I may be good at working a room, networking, driving up sales leads; however, if that is something I find especially draining and I actively look to avoid taking on that responsibility, then it's not my strength. This is important to consider in organizations: Have people been cast in the correct roles? It's not enough to only evaluate an employee's performance to determine if they are in the right role. You should also look at how energized and engaged they are when doing their job.

 Every one of us has strengths—specific areas that are uniquely energizing to us. As a result, it is when we are aware of these strengths and continue to hone them further that we reach our full potential; the opportunity to shift from good to great—and beyond. Gallup refers to this as honing a unique or raw talent into a strength. Talents are naturally reoccurring patterns of thought, feeling, or behavior and can be productively applied. When we take our talents and combine them with knowledge and skill that is practiced, developed, and continually built over time, we create strengths.[30] For example, an employee who has a *talent* of a direct communication style transforms that talent into a *strength* when they know how and when to close the deal and make the sale. To the earlier point, if this employee is also

highly energized by sales, then you have someone well cast in their role. If they are drained by the process of trying to close the deal, despite their talent of being direct, then it is likely that, over time, they will become disengaged in their role.

Why Strengths Matter

A strengths perspective focuses on leveraging one's best qualities, virtues, or characteristics in order to achieve greater success and happiness. Using one's strengths has been shown to increase happiness, engagement, and productivity while decreasing depressive symptoms. Identifying strengths through a strengths assessment and intentionally developing them through application, therefore, is a way to achieve greater effectiveness and happiness. In fact, researchers Seligman, Steen, Park, and Peterson found that people who used their signature strengths of character (from the VIA Survey of Character Strengths) in a new way, for as little as one week, were happier (and less depressed) up to six months later.[31] For example, Pete, when studying in the Master of Positive Psychology program, had this very exercise as homework. So, he chose to leverage one of his signature strengths (from the VIA), Love of Learning, in a new way. So, each morning for a week, rather than check email or watch the news on TV, he would read a research article. Then, he noticed what, if anything, felt different. Pete describes the experience this way: "Those days were just different. I was more creative and my mind was filled with ideas. I just felt more alive."

Now, identify *your* top or signature strengths and find new ways to incorporate them into your daily activities and notice the impact it has on your engagement.

David Cooperrider, known for the development of the change process of Appreciative Inquiry, shared a study of two novice bowling teams. Each was videotaped as they bowled. One group was then coached while viewing a video with the coach pointing out everything they did wrong. For the second group, the coach pointed out everything they were doing right at the moments of improvement. The second group improved by 100 percent more than the first group. Which is the better route to improvement?

Another compelling reason why strengths matter is employee engagement. Remember Tom Rath's research, which showed that when a supervisor focuses on an employee's strengths, the probability of that employee being actively disengaged is only 1 in 100? One percent![32] When it comes to employee engagement, it's clear that not only does this support what we know—feedback is critical—but it shows that that the type of feedback is even more important. What an incredible opportunity to enhance employee engagement by giving strengths-based behavioral feedback.

The Role Strengths Play in Feedback

Before coaches and HRBPs attend our Shift Positive 360 certification, they have a pre-work assignment to complete. We partner them with another participant in the group a few weeks before the training (typically someone they do not know) and ask that they provide each other with three people from their personal or professional network to be interviewed. The interviews are a brief 10–15 minutes and focus on the participants' strengths and what they are like at their best. Then at the certification, the pre-work partners finally get to meet, after having already learned about the other's strengths and when they are at their best. Later when they provide each other the feedback, it's a memorable moment for all, generating lots of positive emotions. We often hear it was a favorite part of the entire certification process. There are a few reasons why this is so.

To be seen through the lens of your strengths and when you are at your best is incredibly meaningful. It allows you to feel seen for who you truly are, at your best and most authentic self. It allows you to feel valued, as if your contributions are impactful and make a difference. It also allows you to feel appreciated, and we know when a person feels appreciated, they are likely to work even harder. A study by online career site Glassdoor revealed that more than 81 percent of employees say they're motivated to work harder when their boss shows appreciation for their work.[33] Are organizations creating enough opportunities to see and recognize people through their strengths?

> To be seen through the
> lens of your strengths and
> when you are at your best is
> incredibly meaningful.

As we mentioned earlier, we often hear from managers that they are good at giving strengths-based feedback already, but what they are really referring to is positive feedback, such as "Great job on the presentation, Kate" or "You're doing well with managing the deadlines—thank you." The former VP of People +

Culture and current Culture + Communication consultant at Bumble, Leah Heck, calls this "candy feedback." When Jen was delivering a keynote at the 2019 Bumble company retreat, Leah explained, "This type of feedback I call candy feedback. It feels good in that brief moment to hear 'great job' yet it doesn't last. We need to give more meaningful feedback that's sustainable." After Bumble heard the keynote, Leah said, "The Shift Positive Method opened people's minds to the power of giving actionable feedback, even when it's difficult. The T-chart method (explained in chapter 5) is now a part of our feedback process, ensuring that conversations are constructive and meaningful."

Positive, or candy, feedback, is simply not enough. Strengths-based feedback goes further: It names something that is unique and specific to that person and illustrates how applying that strength is impactful. This includes saying to a colleague, "Kate, you have a real strength for communication—you have an ability to create a story inside of a pitch deck that not only brings your audience along, but also has the right balance of illustrating the vision while providing just enough detail for proof of concept." This feedback will have a stickiness factor, lasting longer and proving more sustaining for Kate. It helps her not just feel seen and valued, but also points out what to keep doing—more of what is working.

This is one of several reasons to bring more of a strengths-based focus and appreciation to feedback, even at the expense of seeming to focusing on weaknesses. People often believe that if something is not a strength, then it must be a weakness, or something they are bad at. Given our negativity bias, people are likely to obsess over this much more, trying to determine how to improve their weakness, often at the expense of focusing on how to further grow their strengths. Simply put—this is not what will make people more effective.

 We like to refer to the work of Robert Biswas-Diener and his sailboat metaphor when it comes to understanding your strengths in relation to your weaknesses.[34] Consider the two main components of the sailboat—the hull of the ship and the sail. If you have a hole in your hull, that is a weakness. And you need to pay attention to it based on how big it is. If it is a large weakness and water is flowing in, you better bail and fix the leak—fix that weakness. But even if your hull is whole, that doesn't mean you're going anywhere. The sail is your strength. It's what gives you power, movement, and direction.

This is why it's so important to know what your strengths are and how to continuously find new ways to leverage them. In addition to the Shift Positive Method, we like a number of resources for identifying strengths. These include the VIA Survey of Character Strengths, Gallup's CliftonStrengths, and Marcus Buckingham's StandOut strengths assessments. Each one calls attention to your top strengths and provides a helpful report with ideas and tips on how to further develop your strengths.

In any strengths conversation we have with a client, we encourage them to savor what they have learned. Savoring is recognizing, enhancing, and appreciating positive experiences in our lives—or in this case, in ourselves. Research on savoring suggests that practicing savoring is linked to positive outcomes, such as increased happiness and general well-being.[35] Savoring is shown to increase positive affect, optimism, and locus of control while reducing helplessness, depression, and unhappiness.[36] Yet, it can take longer for positive emotions to settle (compared to negative emotions). So, it's important to create the space for savoring—to be intentional about it and slow the pace. It can be powerful for many to read and reread their positive feedback, to truly take in and sit with all the good. For some, it can be more difficult to hear the positive; so, be thoughtful about how you encourage your leaders or team to sit with this feedback. Invite them to embrace this as a healthy dose of self-love and an opportunity to enhance overall well-being.

Whether in a coaching session while reviewing a strengths assessment, in a 360 interview when asking about a leader's strengths, or in a manager training session where each person is sharing their top strengths, inevitably someone will say that a strength can also be a weakness. We are quick to reframe that language by explaining that your strengths are your own unique talents and they are never to be seen as a weakness. However, at times, anyone can overuse a strength to an extent that it may get in the way of effectiveness.

It's helpful to understand the Situational and Social use of strengths as described by Robert Biswas-Diener.[37] Socially, we should be aware of our strengths relative to the others with whom we're interacting and how they might affect that person. A person who is more of an Ideator may drive another who is more of a Critical Thinker nuts. However, there is a situation or a time for brainstorming, ideating, and creative thinking, and then there is a time to think critically, decide, and execute. Being aware of the social fabric and situation at hand really helps refine our perspective on strengths. It is not strengths, strengths, strengths all the time or *inflicting* our strengths on others. Continuing with the metaphor, you need to hoist your sail relative to the conditions so you don't turtle the boat.

Another consideration for the role strengths play in feedback is the concept of priming positive emotions. We learned in the last chapter about Barbara Fredrickson's Broaden & Build Theory—that when we are under the influence of positive emotions, we experience improved visual processing, creativity, resilience, performance, trust, memory for details, and better negotiation and decision-making.[38] Imagine if people had a feedback experience that generated enough positive emotions to empower them to become more effective. When you give real strengths-based feedback, you're naturally able to prime positive emotions in the recipient. This helps to drive a positive mindset when it comes to development goals—the feedback recipient is more likely to feel improvement is possible.

> Imagine if people had a feedback experience that generated enough positive emotions to empower them to become more effective.

Additionally, asking stakeholders about the strengths of the recipient primes the stakeholders to be more open, creative, and able to get past their own negativity bias to create more constructive feedback for the recipient. This leads to our final concept—how to point your strengths toward the areas in which you're trying to be more effective.

Strengths as Doorways to Growth

We were attending a Positive Psychology and coaching workshop put on by an esteemed colleague, Kathleen Stinnett, MCC, and the pre-work required participants to take the VIA Survey of Character Strengths. In looking at the report, which included a ranking of 1–24, we did exactly what we tell our clients not to do: look at what was at the bottom. Jen saw Pete had "curiosity" in his top five; for her it was dead last. Jen was mortified. She thought to herself, *Does this make me a bad coach?*

When it came time to discuss the role of strengths in the workshop, Kathleen asked if anyone would be willing to volunteer for some live coaching on their results. Jen immediately shot her hand up with the hope she could unpack the story she had created around being a terrible coach who lacks curiosity. Jen shared with Kathleen the initial reaction she had to the results and the story she had created. Kathleen, as a great coach would, redirected Jen's attention to the top five strengths on her report. She said, "Jen, if you were to set an intention about becoming more curious, which of your top five strengths could help you to do that?" First, Jen was so relieved Kathleen didn't ask the question, "So, Jen, how could you be more curious?" because Jen already reflected on that and wasn't feeling clear on a path. Jen paused, looking at her report, and said, "Well, number three, perseverance, is what jumps right out at me. Anyone who knows me knows if I say I'll do something, I commit, I follow through, and I never miss a deadline." Kathleen said, "Great. How does that help you become more curious?" Jen went on to explain, "I think I just need to make it a goal and get specific. For 30 days, each morning I'm going to name one thing to be curious about in my day and each evening reflect back on anytime I was curious throughout the day."

After this session, we had an aha moment and came to understand strengths and how to help clients at a whole new level. Beyond the value of leveraging your top strengths to go from good to great and the research showing that using strengths in new ways enhances well-being, there is now another reason.

 If you enter into an area of growth (curiosity) through the doorway of a strength (perseverance), it not only seems more feasible, you're more likely to be successful as a result. The report was true. For Jen, curiosity is not as innate as the other top character strengths: honesty, perspective, and perseverance. So, when she asked herself how to be more curious, she came up blank; it simply wasn't a natural place for her to go. But once she considered leveraging one of her top strengths, perseverance, it not only became clear but also felt doable.

Just because a strength appears at the bottom of the list doesn't mean you are bad at it or that it's not possible to grow that area. This is true for anyone when reviewing a strengths assessment. There is a stacked ranking because the research shows that you're more likely to see more growth and success by focusing on your top 5 or 10—the ones more natural, unique, and energizing for you—than if you focus on the bottom ones. Sure, you may be able to move #24 to #16, but that's far less likely to have the same impact as if you found different ways to further develop and leverage your top strengths.

Jen felt strengthening her curiosity would have a positive impact on her coaching, so as a result, it became a focus for her. In addition, she found a new way to leverage her #3 strength of perseverance. And just like in the sailboat metaphor, your sail gives you power to take you where you want to go. So, in this example Jen is leveraging her strength of perseverance toward an area she'd like to grow: curiosity.

An essential part of the Shift Positive Method is focusing on strengths for all the reasons detailed here and below. It is an incredible gift to help a person to see and discover their own strengths, and then to help them see how those strengths can play an even bigger role in their success, from priming a mindset of possibility to being doorways for growth. This is powerful. As author and speaker Benjamin Zander often says, "power is the ability to empower others." Let's create cultures where we see people through the lens of their strengths, where we give this gift in the form of strengths-based feedback, where we experience the benefits of positive emotions, and finally, where we spend a lot more time savoring the good.

Chapter 4 Recap

❖ Strengths are not what you're good at versus bad at; they are activities that strengthen you, draw you in, and make you feel strong. Using one's strengths has been shown to increase happiness, engagement, and productivity while decreasing depressive symptoms.

❖ Strengths-based feedback is different than positive feedback; it's specific and meaningful and conveys impact. When a supervisor focuses on strengths-based feedback, the likelihood of the employee actively disengaging from their role is only 1 out of 100.

❖ Remember the sailboat metaphor—your strengths are the sail that gives you the power to go where you need to go. Be aware of the extent to which you focus on weaknesses.

❖ It's important to manage your use of strengths situationally and socially, so they don't get in the way of your effectiveness.

❖ Priming positive emotions with strengths-based feedback helps to create a resilient and positive mindset when approaching areas of growth.

❖ Savoring your strengths-based feedback can lead to increased well-being and overall happiness.

❖ When you enter through the doorway of a strength to improve an area of growth, it feels more achievable, making you more likely to create sustainable positive change.

Reflection Prompts:

1. When do you feel your most energized? When do you experience a feeling of flow (when the challenge is high and your level of skill is high as well)? What activities are you doing?

2. Take a few moments to journal five areas that are your strengths and consider new ways you can apply them.

3. What do you see as the strengths of someone close to you? Or of someone you're responsible for providing feedback to? Be specific.

4. How might you or someone you know take a strength and use it as a doorway to a new area of growth?

CHAPTER 5

Growth: Shifting to a Solution-Focused Approach

Traditionally with 360s, once we ask about a person's strengths, we follow it up by asking about weaknesses or "opportunities." So much so that people have come to expect a question about weaknesses in 360s. As explained earlier, we have a negativity bias (negative emotions are stronger than positive emotions), which makes receiving negative feedback more difficult. At the same time, it is what we can be quick to see in others when providing feedback—what's not working; what's broken. This is a bad combination—stakeholders see weaknesses in others quickly, yet receivers are on guard for negative feedback. So, to move from weaknesses to constructive solutions, we need to overcome our biology. How do we do that?

In the Shift Positive Method, we never ask about weaknesses. They may be interesting, insightful, or informative but are insufficient to make change. Instead, we ask people to do some thoughtful work. We ask them to identify what they want the person *to do* rather than not do. It sounds easy, but it takes intention. It can be easy to understand but difficult to practice. Yet, we have a very effective tool to help us do just this. First, however, it's important to understand solution-focused inquiry.

Solution-Focused Inquiry

> "The solution doesn't care why the problem occurred!"

Solution-focused inquiry or solution-focused coaching is an approach focused on searching for solutions rather than focusing on problems. There's a saying in solution-focused coaching, "The solution doesn't care why the problem occurred![39]" This may seem counter-intuitive. Don't we need to fully understand the problem to come up with a solution and avoid it in the future? Not necessarily. That is an assumption—that studying the problem is essential for developing a solution. However, what if we start with the solution? What if we start with the exception to the problem? The problem is not always a problem (a concept of Positive Deviance discussed later). We can ask about potential solutions, or past successes in similar situations, or simply focus on the underlying goal that the person is trying to achieve rather than digging into the problem. Doing this brings more positive affect (remember chapter 3), and therefore more creativity and broader potential solutions, than focusing first and narrowly on the problem. So, does it work?

Thanks to research by Tony Grant,[40] we know that solution-focused coaching leads clients to have better outcomes than problem-focused coaching. With solution-focused coaching, clients experience more positive affect, less negative affect (experiencing negative emotions), greater success in reaching goals, increased self-efficacy, and they generate more action steps to help them achieve their goals. Although real-life coaching conversations are not solely solution-focused or solely problem-focused, agents of change should aim for a solution-focused theme in their work. We're not saying that skill in evaluating problems isn't helpful. Just that we've honed our problem-solving skills for a long time. Now, it is time to hone our solution-building skills and not assume that one is a prerequisite for the other.

In solution-focused coaching and inquiry, we're asking "how" and "what" questions that are focused on potential future solutions and past successes, rather than asking "why" and other questions focused on problems and the past. Here's an immediate example for you: Imagine your boss has stopped by. Notice how it feels when he asks you this question:

"Why aren't you meeting the budget?"

Pause for a moment. Now, notice how it feels if he asks you this instead:

"How can we meet the budget?"

Did you feel a difference? In this very simple example, the first question probably elicited a different feeling than the second. The first makes us feel defensive, at risk. The second makes us physically feel more open, forward-looking, perhaps even supported. Asking, "How could . . . ?" or "What will it take . . . ?" affects us differently than, "What happened?" "Why did it happen?" "Why aren't . . . ?"

In Grant's experiments, problem-focused questions included ones like: How long has it been a problem? How did it start? What are your thoughts about the problem? How do you react to those thoughts? What impact does that have? Whereas, the solution-focused approach was: Think about a possible solution. Imagine it came about. Describe it. How could you start? How do you feel?

This is very significant with respect to setting the tone for constructive feedback and influencing the feedback providers. Rather than asking about weaknesses, we explore questions like "What *do* you want from the client?" and "If she could be even more effective, what would that look like?" "What would it look like if they were even more successful?"

To help us think about solutions or future direction, we like to relay the story told by Szabo and Meier in *Coaching: Plain and Simple*. It's about the possible origins of the term *coach*—a coachman or cab driver taking us from where we are to where we want to go. As said by Fredrike Bannink, solution-focused coach, "When you get into the cab, the driver asks you, 'Where to?' not necessarily 'Where from?'"

What *Do* You Want?

This distinction of looking for what we want rather than what's wrong, or a weakness, is crucial, but not always easy. Take for example Lloyd, who was recently promoted to VP. Lloyd's coach helped him select people who were important to his success, and vice versa, for his 360. One person, Rand, was chosen specifically because he had a difficult relationship with Lloyd. When the coach was interviewing Rand, he came to the question about what would it look like if Lloyd were even more effective.

Rand, in his nice, Minnesotan passive-aggressive way, said, "Well, I think Lloyd should work on trust."

Coach: "Oh, trust? What would that look like?"

Rand: "Well, he has a new team and he should really start building trust with them."

Coach: "Okay, say more."

Rand: "Well, his team and my team really don't have a lot of trust. We should build that trust between them."

The coach continued to ask probing questions about what it would look like, how would Rand know, etc.

Finally, Rand burst out, "I don't trust the guy!"

Coach: "Okay, but what *do* you want?"

Rand couldn't answer the question right away. Instead, he said, "I shouldn't come into the room when his team is there and my team is there and he starts taking the group in a different direction than where I think we should head. He's very good at getting people to follow him and later we need to work our way back so we don't go down a path that I can't agree to. It looks bad that we're not aligned in front of the teams!"

Coach: "That makes sense. Now, I clearly know what you *don't* want him to do. But I still don't know what you want from him instead."

It really took a while for Rand to identify what he wanted. Finally, he looked up and in a stern voice said, "I think he has a pretty good intuition of when we're on the same page and when we're not. So, when that intuition goes off, I want him to pick up the phone and call me or come see me, before we get in the room, so we can be aligned."

Coach: "That's awesome. And what do you think you could do?"

Rand (with a slight grumble): "I could do the same."

This illustrates a couple of very important elements. Even though our approach is called the Shift Positive 360, it is not intended to always be positive or, least of all, fluffy. It is to be constructive—to give specific behavioral information that the client can clearly understand and that the provider can see in their own mind's eye.

Second, this is not always easy. It takes work to identify what we want, rather than what we don't. However, if the coach would have just typed "build trust," that would have left Lloyd wandering in the desert, guessing, and wondering what *to do.* "Build trust" has some fairly accepted definitions, such as: I trust that you'll do what you say you'll do. Or, I trust you because I know you; we've connected personally. What Rand was looking for could also be described as the "no surprises rule." If the coach didn't keep digging, Rand's true intention would have been missed completely.

Even more importantly, Rand wouldn't have noticed it when Lloyd was attempting to build trust. Why? Because of inattentional blindness.

Inattentional Blindness

During our certification training for coaches in the Shift Positive 360, we show a video called the moonwalking bear. The narrator directs the viewer to count how many times the team in white shirts passes the ball. While the team in white is passing the ball, a team with black shirts is passing another ball. At the end of the short video the narrator asks, "Did you get 13?" At that point, individuals in our group start saying, "got it," "nope," "yes." Then the narrator says, "But did you see the moonwalking bear?" Immediately the video rewinds and is played forward again. Now the majority in the room see that, truly, a person in a bear costume had moonwalked directly into the circle of the team in white passing the ball, and then walked out of the circle. People gasp as they realize they never saw a full-grown person in a bear costume on the screen. This illustrates the phenomenon of inattentional blindness. We don't see what we're not looking for.

We also use a picture of a gnarly looking tree with no leaves. We can show it to a group and ask, "How many branches are on this tree?" If we are with a group of engineers, they will literally start counting the number of branches. But usually somebody will speak up and say, "A lot." To which we respond, "Yes, that's the correct answer. There are a lot of branches on this tree." Then we ask, "Now, how many faces are on this tree?" At this point everyone leans forward to look more closely at the tree and we hear them start to count out loud: "Two . . . no four." "I see five." "Wait, there's more." "Yes, there are about 12 or 13 faces on this tree," we respond. To see them, you have to look at the space between the branches. Then the faces begin to reveal themselves. After that, it is almost impossible to look at the tree and not see the faces.

That's what we're doing in the 360 interviews. We're getting people to see what they want rather than what they don't. We're priming them. This is really important because if they can't see the behaviors in their own mind's eye, they won't see it even if the client starts to practice those new behaviors. If they can clearly see the desired behaviors themselves, they will be more likely to notice when they happen. Then they will, almost unconsciously, reinforce them in real time (more about this when we talk about Allies).

> Unless the ally (stakeholder) takes the time to truly think about what success looks like, the client will be guessing, and the ally probably won't recognize it when it does happen.

A footnote to the story about the moonwalking bear: Oftentimes, people in the room may have seen this video before. In fact, some of them may have used it in trainings that they led themselves. So, a little something we like to do while teaching is when Jen is showing the video and subsequently explaining inattentional blindness, Pete will leave the room and change from one brightly colored shirt to a different brightly colored shirt. Pete will return to the front of the room and join in the conversation. A short while later, Jen will ask, "Have you noticed anything else that has changed?" With Pete having been presenting for the good part of a full day by this point, perhaps one person will have noticed that he's changed his shirt. They're simply not looking for it so they don't see it. That is inattentional blindness.

Making the Shift: The T-Chart

So, how do we get to constructive feedback? This takes work on our part as interviewers and feedback providers; we have to dig further. What, specifically, does being a "better communicator" mean? It could mean many things: slowing the pace of delivery, lowering the tone, touching base at least daily, or giving the conclusion first and offering detail only as necessary, etc.

We were told that one of our clients, Troy, talks too much. He interrupts others. He dominates meetings. For Troy, that's useless information. So, we had to dig deeper. "What does 'talking less' look like? What do you want him to do instead?" To that, his stakeholders said things like: "Use active listening skills. Ask others for input. Facilitate. Seek to understand. Be curious; ask questions." At which point, we went even further. "And, what would you notice if he were using active listening skills?"

"He'd pause and paraphrase. He'd ask if I felt understood. He'd say, 'So, what I'm hearing is . . . Is that right?'"

In response, we asked, "If he said, 'So, what I'm hearing is . . . Is that right?' would you notice?" At this point, the response by the stakeholder was, "Definitely. I'd probably fall out of my chair." Then, we know we're there. We've gotten to clear behavioral detail of what *to do*.

Because this can be difficult due to the negativity bias, we use something we call a T-chart. When training a group of people, we ask them to draw a big *T* on a piece of paper. Then, we instruct that the left-hand side is what you want the person to fix, what's broken, what isn't working. We prompt people to notice if their pen is going crazy on this left side (negativity bias). This is the problem-focused side. On the right-hand side, we ask them to write what they want instead. What would it look like? What would they do or say? What would they look like physically? These are some of the prompts that help people to get to the behavioral detail necessary to see it in their own mind's eye. We say, "If you have anything in the right-hand side that includes 'stop,' 'wouldn't,' 'won't,' 'don't,' 'shouldn't,' or any other 'nt's,' then you're not there yet. Keep going."

T-Chart Method	
Problem-Focused	Solution-Focused
Micromanager	Ask curious questions about how I got to my solutions: "Tell me your process for..."
Doesn't trust me to get the job done	Ask about my thinking: "What did you consider to arrive at...?"
Wants it done his way	Let me know when he has confidence in my work. "You've got this and don't need to show me in the future. However, I'd still like to see..."
	Clarify during project kickoffs where he'd like more detail and where we can take more risks.

Whether it's teaching feedback skills or conducing a 360 interview, continuing to ask questions to get to specific, constructive, behavioral detail of what *to do* is a breakthrough for the client and for their stakeholders.

It's Hard to Do Less of a Bad Behavior

Why else is this important? Telling the client what they don't do well or what to stop doing is not very helpful because it's very hard to do "less of a bad behavior." We want to know what the client can do that would be better, instead. Then, by doing more of those behaviors, the client will naturally do less of the behaviors that aren't as effective. Instead of "talking less," "dominates," or "talks too much," it would be "facilitate," "make sure each person is heard," or "ask open-ended questions to increase participation." By doing more facilitating, they'll naturally do less dominating.

It's harder to break
a bad habit than to create
a new one.

Noting What Is Constructive

Whether conducting a training or a Shift Positive 360, a key skill is taking and sharing notes with the client on what is constructive—the solutions, rather than the problems. The Shift Positive Method is not intended to be all positive, but it is intended to be constructive. This takes skill on the part of the interviewer or facilitator to stop typing or writing when the stakeholder is processing what isn't working (left-hand side of the T-chart) and begin taking notes again when they get to what *to do*. We don't take notes on what is broken.

This can be hard as the stakeholder can be stuck on what is broken, what hasn't gone well, or how bad things have really been. A key skill we've learned through practice and error is to pause and simply acknowledge the situation. Pete learned this lesson while interviewing a board member of a nonprofit executive director client of his. He kept reframing and asking, "And what do you want?" Pete even said at one point, "I really don't need to know what wasn't working." To this, the stakeholder replied, "Yes, you need to know. Last year, objectively, was the best year in the organization's history yet almost everyone on the board was ready to resign." To this, Pete realized his error and said, "That sounds really hard. I'm sorry. What would make this year better?" Acknowledging the pain can go a long way in helping the stakeholder move from past challenges to future possibilities.

Getting to the Small Step

 As we get clear about what the stakeholder wants the client *to do*, we ask one more question: "What is one small, achievable step that they can take to move in that direction in the next few months?" This usually elicits a specific behavior or action in the mind's eye of the stakeholder. It may be something the client will say, or a specific action they'll take at a specific time and place, e.g., in the weekly team meeting. The fun thing is that often we even see a physical reaction to the question by the interviewee. They may look up and to the left, deep in thought. Suddenly, they'll look down, make eye contact, and say, "He'd do this . . ." Now, we've primed them to become not just a stakeholder, but an ally, which you'll read about shortly.

This does two things. First, it makes the recommended behavior much easier for the client to understand because it is so specific. Yet, we find, even more importantly, it makes it much more likely for the stakeholder to notice that behavior should the client show it. Then, they'll begin to reinforce the new behaviors, in real time, almost reflexively. A tiny step can have a big impact. When we name a first step, a place to start, an achievable win, we're more likely to keep going toward that vision of more effective.

Two other areas that help a person to grow by looking through the lens of what is working include Positive Deviance and Appreciative Inquiry.

Positive Deviance

Perhaps you've heard the question "When is the problem not a problem?" Positive Deviance (PD) is an approach that looks for the positive outlier among the problems and asks: What happened there? The best story to illustrate this methodology is that of Monique and Jerry Sternin.[41]

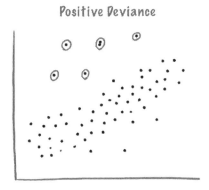

Positive Deviance

In 1990, they were working with Save the Children, a humanitarian aid organization for children. They were asked to help solve a problem of malnutrition in Vietnam. Sixty-five percent of children under age five were suffering from some degree of malnutrition. They were told they had six months to show impact or they would have to leave.

How can just a few people make even a dent in such a problem? How could they dig into such a problem and understand the causes in such a short time? They didn't try. Instead, they used a Positive Deviance approach. First, they had volunteers work with families and weigh children to get a baseline of data. They also noted the level of income in each of those families. They were categorized as poor, very poor, or very, very poor. Then, when they looked at the data, they found something very interesting. Even in the poorest families, there were outliers—kids whose weight was at standard, children who were well nourished despite extreme poverty. So, they knew it was possible.

At first, nothing in the data gave away the solution, until they observed three things these families did differently than most. First, they gathered shrimp, crabs, and snails from the rice paddies and greens from sweet potato tops and added them to the rice. This was considered unusual or even inappropriate, yet it provided protein, iron, and calcium.

Second, these families showed atypically strict hand hygiene— they washed their hands more. Third, usually, families ate meals in the early morning and upon returning from the fields in the evening. In these families, however, children who stayed home to take care of the very young were instructed to feed them four or five times a day in smaller portions. So, those smallest children finished their meals more frequently. They had a solution.

If you had a solution like this, what would you do? Go tell everyone, right? No, they knew that because they were outsiders, that action could be viewed suspiciously. Instead, they invited these families to share their approach with others in the community. By actually seeing individuals from their own community with healthier children, families were influenced and began to take similar steps.

The Sternins were asked to stay beyond the six months. Over a two-year pilot program, malnutrition fell by 80 percent, and over five years, the program was expanded to 250 communities. They are credited with saving tens of thousands of lives, not even counting those to be born to families that had now changed their approach. One of the keys Jerry Sternin describes is "identifying the relevant Positive Deviancy within each local community . . . the community, in other words, cures itself." This points out the value of seeing the community around each client asking, "Where is the problem not a problem?" and creating the solution from within.

Appreciative Inquiry

Similarly, Appreciative Inquiry (AI) builds off of successes to envision an even more effective future. The theory of Appreciative Inquiry was developed by David Cooperrider.[42] Most change methodologies start from the negative perspective—find what is broken and look to create a solution. AI is different; it begins with the positive—what works and what can be learned from that to create more success. It is about intentionally crafting a desired future. In feedback, we're talking about crafting a desired future between the client and stakeholders. If they could be even more effective together, what would that be like?

Traditional problem-solving (deficit-based) approaches include: identifying the problem; conducting a root cause analysis; brainstorming solutions and analyzing alternatives; then, developing treatment or action plans. Appreciative Inquiry (strengths-focused innovation) is different. It uses the 4-D approach: Discover the best of what is; dream what might be; design what should be; and deliver what will be.

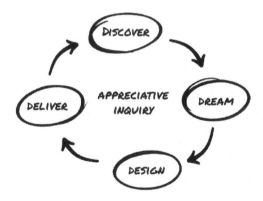

What's fascinating are the assumptions of Appreciative Inquiry. Try to translate them into the context of gathering feedback. Cooperrider, Whitney, and Stavros lay out these assumptions:

❖ In every organization, something works.

❖ The moment we ask a question it influences the group.

(So, crafting our questions is critical to the process of asking for feedback.)

❖ Become obsessed with learning from our successes.

❖ We can feel more confident about the future when we know what we do well or have done well in the past. We can carry forward the best of the past.

❖ Under the influence of positive emotions, we become more creative.

But does AI work? Research on the Appreciative Inquiry approach has found that change is most effective when focused on changing how people *think*.[43] That's why a coach is instrumental in helping change the interviewees' way of thinking, e.g., influencing interviewees to envision what they want, rather than priming them to see what's broken.

Similar to Appreciative Inquiry, in the interviews, we want to learn from past successes and envision a compelling future between the client and stakeholder. We want to explore a time when the stakeholder and the client have been really successful in the past—a problem they solved or a project they worked on. We want to understand what happened and the underlying supports that made that success possible. Why? Because, if they can understand and make those underlying supports happen more frequently, then it's likely that they will have more successful experiences in the future. These supports may be things like starting early, having a clear goal, and sharing budget or resources, as well as things like "we had some very straightforward conversations early on; we took shared ownership of the outcome; I adapted to his direct style and didn't take it personally."

For example, Ben. Jen was asked to coach him because his team "no longer wanted to follow him up the mountain." So, when she asked each of his direct reports to share a time when they worked well with Ben, several called out one specific advertising campaign. During that time, Ben managed his team differently. "He gave us more space and time to create." "We felt a greater sense of ownership knowing we had responsibility for a specific part of the campaign." "We had clear check-in dates and Ben didn't bother us for updates in between." The team was able to name the behaviors from Ben that helped them to be their best and that they wanted more of in the future. During the debrief, Ben too recalled how well that specific campaign had gone. He realized how he had shown up and had a clear understanding of what his team was looking for.

Additionally, we ask about the strengths that the client brought to the situation *and* the strengths that the stakeholder brought to the situation. Here the coach pays close attention to the strengths of the stakeholder for a specific reason, which we'll explain in chapter 6.

The critical element that leads to growth for the client is the ability to garner constructive, solution-focused feedback. This takes practice by the coach to develop the reflex of reframing; to hear what is broken and help the feedback provider reframe it to a behavior that is beneficial. The more one is exposed to solution-focused inquiry, Positive Deviance, and Appreciative Inquiry, and understands inattentional blindness, the more readily this happens. However, this doesn't happen alone. In the next chapter, stakeholders become allies.

Chapter 5 Recap

❖ We never ask about weaknesses. They may be interesting, insightful, or informative but are insufficient to make change. We need to go further.

❖ We need to identify what the stakeholder wants the client *to do* rather than not do.

❖ In solution-focused inquiry, there's a saying: "The solution doesn't care why the problem occurred!"

❖ The distinction of looking for what we want rather than what's wrong, or a weakness, is crucial but not always easy. So, we can employ the T-chart method to help move from the problem-focus to the solution-focus.

❖ Unless the stakeholder takes the time to truly think about what success looks like, the client will be guessing, and the stakeholder probably won't recognize it when it does happen.

❖ Due to inattentional blindness, we often miss what we're not looking for. So, we want to prime the stakeholder to clearly see in their mind's eye what they want instead in behavioral detail.

❖ It's hard to do less of a bad behavior. So, we want to identify more effective behaviors, such that by doing more of those behaviors, the client will naturally do less of the behaviors that aren't as effective.

❖ We don't take notes on weaknesses or what is broken. Acknowledging what is hard goes a long way. Shift Positive isn't intended to be all positive, but it is intended to be constructive.

❖ The more specific we can get the stakeholder to be about a "small step" for the client to take, the more vividly they see it and the more likely they will notice it when it happens.

❖ Positive Deviance asks, "When is the problem not a problem?" It focuses on the positive outlier rather than digging into problems. It assumes that the solution will come from the community itself.

❖ Similarly, Appreciative Inquiry focuses on change by discovering the best of what is, dreaming what might be, designing what should be, and delivering what will be. With feedback, this helps us begin to craft an even better future between the stakeholder and client.

Reflective Prompts:

1. Notice how you hear feedback from your inner critical voice. Try reframing it and ask what you could you do instead. What would success look like?

2. Think of someone who you can provide feedback on, practice with the T-chart (a worksheet is available in the appendix), and see how you can move from problem-focused to solution-focused, being clearer and more specific on the solution side.

3. Once you complete a T-chart exercise, consider one small step you can name for that person to focus on first.

4. Remembering Positive Deviance and Appreciative Inquiry, consider a common problem in your workplace. Now, where is there an exception to the issue? Where is the problem not a problem? Look deeper; what makes it so?

CHAPTER 6

Allies: Building a People System of Support

As we discussed in chapter 3, we don't change by ourselves. We are influenced by those around us. When trying to sustain change, we benefit from creating a people system of support—people aware of our goals and actively participating in our development. We like how this is articulated in the book *Big Potential*, where Shawn Achor summarizes: "almost every attribute of your potential—from intelligence to creativity to leadership to personality and engagement—is interconnected with others. We need to stop trying to be faster alone, and start working to become stronger together."

> "We need to stop trying to be faster alone, and start working to become stronger together."

This brings us to one of our most significant beliefs about feedback: Effective feedback is not a process of gathering and giving information to a client. It is a process of nudging people in the client's human system to see what they truly appreciate about the client, what the client can do to be even more effective, and even more, to see how the change in that client is in relationship with and critically tied to themselves.

To support this viewpoint, we'll review the relational aspect of feedback and the importance of social support. We will detail the process of turning stakeholders into allies and how this creates a shift from one-way feedback to two-way accountability. Finally, we'll look at the necessity of transparency over confidentiality.

Feedback Is Relational

In their article "The Feedback Fallacy,"[44] Buckingham and Goodall make compelling, scientifically supported arguments about the misconceptions of feedback. One, they explain that feedback is relational and always relative to the person who is providing it, meaning it is not fact-based or objective. So, "all we can do is share our own feelings and experiences, our own reactions." That is, how the other person's behaviors impact us. Therefore, feedback statements are not truth, but only *our* truths.

Two, they point out that neurons grow where we already have the most neurons, meaning our brain grows where it is already strongest. Therefore, "focusing people on their shortcomings doesn't enable learning; it impairs it." Critical feedback inhibits neural circuits. Conversely, they say, paying attention to strengths creates learning—we should notice when someone behaves in a way that positively impacts us and point it out to them in the moment. Again, this points out how feedback is relative to the person providing it. They end with a wonderful summary statement, "We excel *only* when people who know us and care about us tell us what they experience and what they feel, and in particular when they see something within us that really works."

So, feedback is not truth; it is perspective—another person's perspective of you. It is all relative to them and what is important to them. They can only tell you how they see you, experience you, and what they feel. This is valuable—it tells you how you can be more effective with *them*; it is not the truth about what is better. It is merely a clue about what is better for them. Often, however, they don't realize that their feedback to you is merely relative to themselves. Further, they often don't know what they actually do want from you; they can only see what doesn't work well for them.

To illustrate how feedback is actually about the perception and relationship dynamics between two people, we'll share the story of Cassie, vice president of Regulatory Affairs at a medical supply company. The company was headed by an all-male executive team. Pete, the coach, was interviewing Bobby, a peer to Cassie's boss, who was also on the executive team. Pete asked how Cassie might be even more effective in the future.

Bobby responded, "Well, she'd be a little less emotional . . ." As he said this, his voice trailed off as if he had made a realization. Pete let the comment hang in the air for a while.

Then, Bobby spoke again. "My wife is a professional in a male-dominated organization. If she ever heard me say something like that . . ."

Pete responded, "So how would you like to perceive Cassie in the future?"

Bobby thought for a moment and then responded, "I'll take someone with her passion seven days a week over someone who doesn't give a shit!"

From that point on, Bobby became one of Cassie's biggest allies, and his social support was instrumental in her professional development.

Social Support

Incredibly, having social support helps us to see challenges in a more moderate way—it is central to achievement of long-term positive change. Experiments have shown that our physiological resources, such as physical fitness, age, and feeling physically refreshed, influence our visual perception. That is, when we feel our physical resources are depleted, hills appear steeper and distances appear greater. At the same time, people who feel physically rested and in shape, or who are young, will see a hill as less steep.

> "Having social support helps us see challenges in a more moderate way."

So, researchers Schnall, Harber, Stefanucci and Proffitt[45] asked the question, "How about psychosocial resources: social support?"

Would that affect a person's visual perception of a slope? They ran experiments. Their findings were telling. Participants accompanied by a friend, when standing in front of a hill, estimated the hill to be 10 to 20 percent less steep than participants who were alone (even though the friend was standing three feet away, facing the other way, and not talking—just standing there). In further experiments, they found just having people *think* of a "supportive person" led participants to see a hill as 10 to 20 percent less steep.

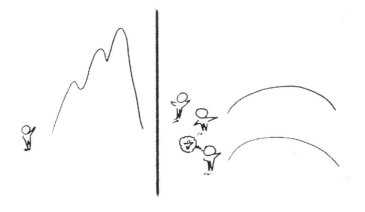

Through other research, we know that the mere presence of another person can be beneficial, especially if the person provides non-evaluative and nondirective support. This "buffering hypothesis"[46] shows that social support is protective against the common cold[47], heart disease[48], and even cancer[49]. Further, the relationship quality is important. When the perceived closeness, warmth, or positive regard for our support person increases, our perceived steepness of the hill decreases.

We love the authors' note as they conclude their article:

> "If social support, opportunities for emotional disclosure, and differences in hope, optimism, self-worth, and self-efficacy cause people to see challenges in a more moderate way, then people who enjoy these resources will live in a subjectively less demanding and less stressful world. Conversely, those deprived of such resources will live in a world where hills are steeper, distances greater, precipices deeper, and other kinds of physical challenges more daunting and demanding."

Simply put, we want to encourage cultures where people feel their challenges are less demanding and stressful by creating social support around them. Especially when it comes to growth and development. But that takes engagement and effort from more than just the client.

Change Blindness

Remember that Marshall Goldsmith and Howard Morgan found that one variable emerged as central to the achievement of positive long-term change with coaching: the client's ongoing interaction and follow-up with colleagues. Even more, change blindness, a phenomenon similar to inattentional blindness, leads stakeholders to miss entirely the client's new behaviors as they occur, because they are not actively looking for them. So, if colleagues are not actively engaged, they won't notice when the client does change.

Therefore, the client might begin working hard to make changes; however, if people in the system are not looking for, noticing, and recognizing the changes, they may soon fade. It is very easy for stakeholders to continue to see the client the way they always have—through old filters. That makes it much more difficult for the client to make progress. As said earlier, it is an error to return a changed person to an unchanged system and expect the changes to stick. Or, as said by our friend Jess Amortegui in a more entertaining way, "You can't put a cucumber in a jar of vinegar and expect it to keep from becoming a pickle." How do we influence each other?

Positive Reinforcement and the Influence We Have on Each Other

Mr. Schaeffer was Pete's seventh grade science teacher. He was a tall man with who walked with a brace on his arm and leg and who had a large scar on his head. No one really knew why. However, it gave him a striking and daunting persona. At the time, the teacher throwing an eraser at your head was not uncommon—and probably for good reason. One day, the class decided to run their own experiment. This time on Mr. Schaeffer.

Before he came into the room, the class decided to try to get Mr. Schaeffer, who stood behind a long table at the front of the room, to walk over to his right and put his hand on the waste basket. So, when Mr. Schaeffer moved a step to his right or gestured in that direction, every kid in class would sit forward in their chair ever so slightly. When he moved back to his left, they sat back. To the right, they went forward. To his left, back. Slowly and gently, he got closer and closer to the waste basket to his right. Finally, as he hovered near the garbage can, he dropped his hand on the silver swinging lid and the class erupted in laughter. Recognition and reinforcement are powerful tools for change. Now, how can we take this lesson from the classroom to the workplace?

From Stakeholders to Allies—"One Thing"

We hardly consider the ways in which we influence each other every day. When we turn and look a person in the eyes, it impacts them differently as compared to when we continue to look at the computer screen. When we ask an open-ended question in follow-up to something our significant other has said, it helps them feel seen and heard, and influences them to keep sharing their story. These nudges are powerful and happen all day long.

So, we want to nudge our client's people system to move from being *stakeholders*, offering feedback, to becoming *allies*, offering positive reinforcement and becoming partners in our client's development. We can work on behalf of our client to enlist each person we interview to be part of the client's support system. To do this, we ask the interviewee to be an ally, to offer one specific thing that they will do to help the client be more successful.

Furthermore, we can build off of the ally's strengths that we discovered earlier. We help the ally identify "one thing" that they can do to help the client grow. Marti was a client of ours—a large and very tall man who was also very analytical and introverted. Due to this, he walked looking down, often lost in thought, and was described as the "grumpy bear." The feedback being given to him by the head of investor relations was that he should project more in meetings and make eye contact, especially when making presentations to the board audit committee. This was anxiety-producing for him. The person offering this feedback was an energetic man who himself really enjoyed presenting. However, during the interview he disclosed that it wasn't always the case. He had worked for years to get more comfortable presenting, had grown to actually liking it, and become rather good at it. So, his "one thing" was to be Marti's "presentation partner." He committed to continuing to talk with Marti about Marti's approach to presenting, watch for him to look up from his notes and make eye contact with the CEO and finance chair, watch their reactions, share his observations, and then reinforce what was working.

If we can enroll each interviewee to commit to doing one thing to support our client, by the conclusion of the Shift Positive 360 process, the client will have six, eight, ten, or twelve people in their system all willing to help them—committed allies. In this way, success happens much more quickly. Imagine how it would feel to have people you know who are willing to help—to be there with you and reinforce the steps you take in your development.

 It usually is not a large commitment on the part of each person. Simply promising to look for and recognize when they see the client attempting new behaviors—offering recognition and feedback along the way—is huge reinforcement. Or, the person may commit to bringing up a difficult topic, providing mentoring in a specific area, or offer to debrief after important meetings. The closer the "one thing" is to the ally's own strengths, the easier it is for them to commit to and the more likely they'll follow through.

Even more energizing, in some interviews, the ally comes to realize how the behavior of the client is intertwined with and perhaps even caused by their own behaviors. Exposing these dynamics and having a big "aha" is wonderful to witness. Case in point: Maxwell was CEO of a medical service owned and shared by several hospitals. (Often, hospitals compete with each other. However, because this particular medical service is quite expensive, the hospitals are collaborative members of the business.) Dan, the board chair and a renowned chief medical officer at one of the metropolitan hospitals, was asked by the coach what "one thing" he could do to support Maxwell.

Dan explained, "Well, you need to understand the life cycle of the organization. When we hired Maxwell, operations were in shambles, finances were very poor, the leadership team needed to be upgraded, and safety needed to become paramount. He's done that. He's great at putting the operations in order, he has a strong team, services and finances are up, and the culture is founded on safety. Now, he needs to shift—to focus on the member hospitals—where should we grow and what are their needs? Health care reform is impacting reimbursement and we need to know how to adjust. Basically, become externally focused."

Coach: "And what can you do to help?"

Dan: "Well, currently I talk with him at least weekly, and once a month we sit down and have breakfast together. Even though

I am moving out of the chair role, I'm happy to continue to connect with him."

Coach: "So, what do you talk about in your meetings?"

Dan: "I ask him about the services, how the finances are looking, and how staff are doing."

With a raised eyebrow, the coach asked, "Do you think he prepares for those meetings?"

As it dawned on Dan, he said, "I'm sure he does. I'm the problem, aren't I?"

Coach: "So, what might you do in the future instead?"

Dan: "I can ask him about the membership, where he's visited, what he's learning about reimbursement, potential hospital systems to add from the five-state region, and how to navigate those conversations."

Simply by changing his questions, Dan went on to have a huge impact on Maxwell. This is a case that clearly illustrated how the behaviors of the client were actually in response to the behaviors of the ally. Often, for the client to change, the ally needs to change as well.

Allies Aren't Always Allies . . . to Start

As mentioned in chapter 5, selecting stakeholders is very important. We want to select those who are most important to the client's success and for whom the client is important to their success. This means people are being interviewed who may have a very difficult relationship with the client. We do this intentionally because our role as coach is to nudge each person whom we interview to become part of our client's growth and development—to move them to allyship. We are going to work on our client's behalf to actually help improve that relationship.

During the interview, this can be difficult. We may need to challenge the stakeholder to become an ally by stating, "Don't expect change to happen unless you're willing to be a part of it." At times, this can be a very modest action like affirmatively connecting with the client, having a meal together, or beginning to communicate again. As said earlier, the Shift Positive 360 is not intended to be all positive, but it is intended to be constructive.

> The Shift Positive 360 is not intended to be all positive; it is intended to be constructive.

From One-Way Feedback to Two-Way Accountability

Traditionally, 360s are conducted at one point in time, and then the stakeholder involvement is over. That's not the case with the Shift Positive 360. It marks the beginning of the ally's involvement with the client—the beginning of two-way accountability.

At the close of the interview, the coach lets the ally know that the client will likely follow up to thank them, involve them in their development goals, and talk with them about the "one thing" they've offered to do. The coach lets the ally know that they may also receive a progress survey during the middle and/or end of the client's coaching that will not just ask about progress, but how they have supported the client along the way.

Right after the interview in the Shift Positive 360, the coach sends an email highlighting the "small step" the ally recommended for the client and the "one thing" they've committed to doing to support the client. So in the earlier story, the coach sent Dan a follow-up email with his own language stating the small step he suggested for Maxwell (the client getting the 360) and the "one thing" he could do as an ally to support Maxwell's development.

Small Step: *Shift focus to membership.*

One Thing: *In our meetings, I can ask him about the membership: who he's visited, what he's learning about the impact of changes with reimbursement, potential expansion in the five-state region, and how to navigate those conversations.*

This further primes the ally to look for changes and formalize the role they may play in the client's development plan.

The client's professional development plan also keeps the allies involved. Traditional development plans include focus areas, activities, and measures of success and progress. The Shift Positive approach goes further to also include the strengths of the client and how those will be leveraged toward areas of growth. Even more, it overtly states the name of each person who was interviewed and the "one thing" they've committed to do to support the client. That way, the HR business partner or coach can return frequently to ask how they are continuing to engage their allies to support their development progress.

Shift Positive 360®

Name	Maxwell	**Title** CEO
Organization	MedServ	**Date** 1/18/23

development goals	actions	strengths to leverage
Brief descriptions of my leadership development goals	Specific action(s) I will take for my development during my coaching engagement	Strengths to leverage against these goals
• Shift focus to be external – focus on members	• Visit bases • Evaluate expansion • Conversations about changing reimbursement • Devise vision for expansion & cost management	• Intellectual curiosity • Knowledge of the field • Relationships across the healthcare system

Coaching Plan

Identify 2-3 development goals. Then identify specific actions, outcomes, strengths and support that align with your goals.

allies + support	success measurement	progress
How my allies will support my progress and any additional support needed	Desired outcomes / measures of success	Summary of what's been completed, what's working, specific wins, or what needs to shift
• Dan – regularly ask about external focus: membership, visits, reimbursement, expansion, key conversations.	• Recommendations for expansion • Bring members together to create strategy for managing shared services • Feedback to board from members that they feel aligned around a shared vision	• First conversation with Dan about reimbursement • Expansion committee formed

Measuring Progress

Next, our approach utilizes a progress survey. In it, the client specifically lists their behavioral development goals. The progress survey is designed to take Marshall Goldsmith and Howard Morgan's research one step further. Their research showed that a client's interaction and follow-up with colleagues (termed the "follow-up factor") resulted in striking improvement. We believe allies' commitment ("one thing") to the client will correlate even further with improvement in the client's development. The more the allies follow through on their commitments, the more likely they'll perceive growth in the client. Further, the survey clearly identifies progress by the client, what is working well, what they recommend the client continue to do, what they've done to support the client, how frequently they did their "one thing," how they will continue to support the client going forward (re-enroll their support), and the ROI or impact of the client's progress on the business. This is also useful to determine the impact of coaching and other leadership development activities, and may be repeated over the course of the coaching engagement.

Recently, a coach was sitting with his CFO client and the CEO. They were reviewing a Shift Progress Survey that showed marked improvement in his development areas. However, when it came to the involvement of his teammates, the results were disappointing. Only "very infrequently" did his allies follow through on their commitments or the "one thing" they promised to do in support of the client. To this, the CEO commented, "We failed you. You worked really hard on your development and we let you down. We didn't hold up our end of the bargain and commitments we made to you. This approach is different—it is about our support of one another. We'll talk about our responsibility to each other at our next executive committee meeting."

What a powerful sentiment and endorsement of social support from that CEO. This is the opportunity—to shift an entire culture so that people become allies in each other's development.

Transparency over Confidentiality

By this point you may be wondering: How can all of this specific behavioral feedback and social support be understood if it is confidential? The answer is, it's not confidential. Confidentiality is a symptom of a broken system. We have a saying: "When we don't know how to say something constructively, we say it confidentially."

> "When we don't know how to say something constructively, we say it confidentially."

Since feedback is relative to the specific person providing it, not fact-based or objective, it therefore cannot be confidential and also be effective. Further, because this is a solution-focused approach, it is not intended to be confidential or anonymous. Rather, understanding the context of the feedback gives the client the best opportunity to understand the desires of others, be versatile in their approach with others, and therefore be more effective. Context matters—different people are looking for different things.

Even more, because the feedback is solution-focused and notes are taken only on what *to do* or what the client's "next" might be, it is actually unnecessary for the feedback to be confidential. We are teaching people through the interview to shift from problem-focus to solution-focus and to name desired behaviors. Because of this, they don't mind the transparency. In fact, they feel quite proud when we read a response back to them knowing they have provided such useful and clear feedback. Interestingly, the people who tend to have the greatest difficulty accepting this transparency are HR or L&D professionals. Confidentiality is such an accepted practice with feedback methods that it takes a moment to adjust. If we dig a little to understand why confidentiality was designed into feedback systems—the negativity bias—we can see that it is no longer necessary and is detrimental to a strengths-based and solution-focused approach.

Those being interviewed rarely have any hesitancy over their responses not being confidential. It helps to frame the Shift Positive 360 at the beginning by saying, "Don't worry, I'll never ask you what the client isn't good at or weaknesses. I will ask you to work a little harder and think about what, specifically, they can do to be even more effective. Further, if you ever get stuck or want to say something but don't know how, just say it and we'll figure it out together before I put it down. I want you to be comfortable with what I share. I'll repeat or summarize for you what I'm hearing as we go along or at the end so that you're comfortable with what I type and that they'll read."

By the conclusion of the interviews or facilitation using the Shift Positive Method, the ally often states, "I have no problem sharing this with the client. You've helped me put into words what I now feel comfortable saying directly." Recently, one of our favorite comments at the close of an interview was, "These are things I could and should have said to him myself. Yet, we don't take an hour to think about each other and offer how we can benefit each other."

In our approach, the only person who receives a copy of the Shift Positive 360 report is the client, as this is intended to be developmental, not evaluative or used for compensation or promotion decisions. This also allows the allies to not be distracted by who they think will read the report or how it might be used, and keeps people from cherry-picking stakeholders who'll only say good things about them. Further, there is no summary from the interviews. The comments are shared directly. Why? In our experience, we found that when a coach distills the interviews into a summary, categories, or key findings, they are running it through their own filters. This is wrong because the coach is not "in" the system of the client. They don't live in their client's world. We found that the client may be very interested in a particular point or comment that the coach could have glossed over and, conversely, well aware of a point that the coach thought very important.

Finally, as said earlier, context matters. There are no averages to behaviors. There is no "5" on a 10-point scale for the competency of "communication," "strategic agility," or "organizational savvy" (whatever that is). A client's direct report may really appreciate that they give lots of detail, while their peer would like to see them start with the headline or conclusion during executive committee meetings and hold the detail for questions should they come.

This doesn't mean there isn't a lot of communication. To the contrary. Once the client creates their development plan, we encourage them to share it with their boss or board, peers, and direct reports. Again, the goal is to create a people system of support where each ally is engaged in the leader's development. How else can we help a client grow? By understanding how their energy affects others, which we'll explore next in chapter 7.

Chapter 6 Recap

❖ We don't change by ourselves. Therefore, constructive feedback is not a process of gathering and giving information to a client. It is a process of nudging people to move from being stakeholders to becoming allies.

❖ Feedback is relational and always relative to the person who is providing it, not fact-based or objective. Therefore, eliciting change in another requires effort and commitment by oneself.

❖ Social support helps us see challenges in a more moderate way.

❖ The client may be working hard to make changes; however, if people are not looking for, noticing, and recognizing changes, they may soon fade.

❖ Recognition and positive reinforcement are powerful tools for change and we influence each other in small ways every day.

❖ We want to nudge our client's human system to move from being stakeholders offering feedback to becoming allies partnering in their development. We do this by asking for the person to identify "one thing" they'll do, specifically, to support the client in their development. In this way, we move from one-way feedback to two-way accountability.

❖ The Ally stays engaged beyond the interview as part of the client's ongoing development plan, in response to the progress survey, and in carrying through on their "one thing" commitment to the client.

❖ The Shift Positive Method is not confidential. Confidentiality is unnecessary and even detrimental in a strengths-based, solution-focused approach. Transparency is crucial because context matters as feedback is relative to the specific person providing it.

Reflection Prompts:

1. Think about feedback you have for someone. Consider how it is relational and relative to you and your preferences. How can you get clearer on what it is that *you* specifically need or want from them? Can you recognize that as your perspective, not necessarily truth?

2. How can you offer support the next time you provide feedback? Consider the person for whom you did the T-chart exercise on in chapter 5. Ask yourself: *What's one thing I can do to support their growth?*

3. What comes up for you as you consider eliminating confidentiality from feedback?

CHAPTER 7

How Energy Impacts the System

If constructive feedback is relative to the person providing it and allies influence change in the client, how then does the client affect the allies? What is the client's impact on the people system? Consider this:

What does it feel like when someone walks into the room? Or when you see a certain name pop up on your phone? What impact does it have on you? How does it affect *your* energy? Perhaps you feel a heaviness in your chest, you sigh, and you realize you just don't have the mental energy to have a conversation with them because it's always negative and feels draining.

We all have people in our lives who affect our energy in positive ways—and at times in negative ways. Perhaps you sit down to craft an email to someone who has a tendency to take things personally and often overreacts. You notice your heart beats a bit faster as you fill in the "to" field of the email. You begin typing, hit delete, then start retyping something new, trying to figure out how to say it in a way that won't prompt a dramatic reaction. Afterward, you may feel tired, as if it's zapped your energy.

We simply feel others as their energy comes into our space. We open up or we close down in response. Also, the same person can have a different impact on us depending on how they show up in that moment—a quick staccato walk, small grunts and humphs, or a slow yet light air about them. Social network analysis helps us understand this effect.

Social Network Analysis

Social network analysis (or organizational network analysis) is a field of study that looks at how people are connected to each other. It is a way of looking at the relationships between individuals within organizations and other social systems such as schools, communities, etc. When used in an organization, we can ask a number of questions such as: Who do you go to for information? Who do you like to work with? What information do you read? With whom do you do projects? Who helps you solve problems? Who do you like on your team?

Utilizing social network analysis, the results of these questions are then put through a software application that creates a three-dimensional picture of the way people are connected to each other. In the picture, dots represent individual people and lines represent the connections between them. Then, visually, you can see how people are interconnected. Insight—it looks nothing like an organizational chart. That's simply not how we get work done. Instead, we seek out those people who can be most helpful (and avoid those who are not).

This tool can be helpful in evaluating, for example, how a merger is progressing. Are people coming together and forming multiple links across the organizations? Are there specific people that others are relying on to get their work done? Are silos evident? Are new teams forming? We can identify points of risk, uncover impediments, and identify people that are very important to the system. It provides a visual representation of the people system that otherwise isn't easily seen.

Within social network analysis, one question is highly predictive of performance and future leadership: "Who do you go to for information?" Information holders and providers are very valuable. However, there's another question that is four times as predictive of performance and future leadership: *"**When you interact with this person, how does it affect your energy?**"*[50] This makes common sense. We share information, brainstorm, problem-solve, and innovate with those who energize us.[51] We get more done with people who raise our energy; those with whom we enjoy engaging—who bring us up even if the problem is a tough one. We still come away feeling respected and thinking that the interaction was productive and worthwhile, even if hard. These energizers do well and rise rapidly in organizations. Note, this doesn't mean they are highly energetic people. Rather, we simply find engaging with them to be energizing to us.

In his book *Practicing Positive Leadership*, Kim Cameron states, "The findings from this study[52] revealed that when individuals are exposed to a positively energizing leader in their workplace, they have significantly higher personal well-being, higher satisfaction with their jobs, higher engagement in their organization, higher job performance, and higher levels of family well-being than those without exposure to positively energizing leaders. Moreover, the organizational unit in which these people work has significantly more cohesion among employees, more orientation toward learning, more expression of experimentation and creativity, and higher levels of performance than units without an energizing leader. The impact of having an energizing leader at work, in other words, was found to be extremely strong."

> "The impact of having an energizing leader at work was found to be extremely strong."

Cameron goes on to say, "Studies confirm that individuals who positively energize others are higher performers themselves.[53] Moreover, positively energized people are more adaptive, more creative, suffer from fewer physical illnesses and accidents, and experience richer interpersonal relationships than others. People tend to avoid and limit their communication with de-energizers, whereas they are attracted to positive energizers."[54] This provides fertile ground for exploring our client's effect on the energy of others.

Application

When gathering feedback, we like to use the energy question (*When you interact with this person, how does it affect your energy?*) because it is so understandable and immediately relatable. After asking the question, we give a further explanation:

"Have you ever had a situation where you stood outside somebody's office and had to think about what you were going to say before going in because you were concerned how the person might react? Or, you've spent 10 minutes typing a three-sentence email to get it 'just right' so that the other person wouldn't take it the wrong way? There is something about that person, or how they're showing up that day, that makes you hesitate or that drains your energy."

Here's the important part:

"Of course, all of us have behaviors that bring people up and others that bring people down. I want my client to understand how they impact others' energy, and specifically what they do that raises people's energy and what do they do that drains or zaps people's energy."

We've found something interesting after using the energy question thousands of times. The same behavior that raises one person's energy will zap another person. It is easy to see in the introvert/extrovert dynamic—the extrovert can overwhelm the introvert and the introvert can seem hesitant to the extrovert. However, we've found many specific ways that can be immediately helpful to the client.

For example, Holly was the business unit president for small appliances. Joe reported to the VP of Direct-to-Consumer Sales, Holly's peer. Holly was very important to Joe's success (and vice versa) because they had a stretch goal to double direct-to-consumer sales of small appliances in two years. Joe wanted to know how he could be more effective working with Holly. So, he chose her to be one of his Shift Positive 360 stakeholders.

During the interview, the coach asked Holly, "When you interact with Joe, how does it affect your energy?"

Holly gave a general response—that she appreciated Joe's diligence and felt confident that Joe knows his stuff and she found that energizing. When probed to go further about what Joe did specifically that raised Holly's energy and what he did that drained her energy, some really useful insights came out.

"I love it when Joe gives me the bottom line without all the detail, but, I hate it; I mean hate it when Joe says, 'I don't know right now so let me look into it and get back to you.'"

This is where it gets really interesting. We want to understand the specifics that can be draining for a colleague. Who would have known that saying you'll look into something would be draining?

Holly went on to say, "By saying that, Joe cuts me out. It stops the conversation and I'm left hanging."

At this point, it is usually easy to reframe allies to be clear on what they want versus what they don't and often the ally reframes themselves, as Holly did. She continued, "I just want him to share with me his first reaction—I won't hold him to it. But I want to know how he'll think about the problem. Then, I can be part of it and help influence how he'll think it through."

This was incredible information for Joe. First, let's understand the dynamics of the two people through the lens of Insights Discovery, a personality assessment. This tool uses a circle that is divided into four colors to describe personality: fiery red (driver style), sunshine yellow (expressive), cool blue (analytical), and earth green (relational). Joe is very Analytical, or leads with Blue, while Holly leads with Yellow/Red—Expressive/Driver. Basically, their personality styles are the opposite. Joe wants to be accurate; Holly is direct, wants to engage, be part of it, and move forward.

So, what did Joe do with this information? The very next meeting, when Joe felt the urge to say, "Let me look into that and get back to you," he paused and said, "I don't know the answer right now, but this is how I'd think it through . . . ." To which, Holly smiled and said great and then offered her own thinking on how much detail was necessary and what she thought of the situation.

Behind the Curtain

This example illustrates many key points. First, versatility is important. Being behaviorally specific allows the client to resp ond or interact with different people in different ways. Having utilized many different personality assessments (social styles, colors, MBTI, Enneagram, etc.), the one thing that has stuck with us is that there is little correlation between style and success. However, there is a high correlation between versatility and performance. The more one person can understand another's style, truly appreciate that person's style, and then modify their own behavior to put that other person at ease (versatility), the more comfortable and productive they become together. The energy question gives people specific behavioral information to help them be more versatile.

Second, asking about what zaps or drains the ally's energy runs the risk of being "negative" toward the client. However, framing it in the way we do—"we all have behaviors that raise others' energy and those that drain them—and the same behavior can raise some and drain others"—helps the ally be specific and constructive. Further, by this point in the Shift Positive 360 interview, we find that the ally has learned to reframe *themselves*. The point being, we are teaching the stakeholders to become allies by learning to reframe themselves from what they *don't* want to what they *do* want. The sneaky truth is that we are nudging and teaching each interviewee to reframe to solutions; to see the faces between the branches. That way, a small smile will cross their face the first time they see the new behavior in the client, which will reinforce and increase the probability of it happening again.

Also, with regard to this energy question being "negative," in our experience, we find that the client is usually even harder on themselves. When we are interviewing the client as part of the Shift Positive 360, we ask how they think they impact the energy of others. They really appreciate having the specific information that helps them become more versatile with each individual person being interviewed.

Just as the allies impact the behavior of the client, so too does the client impact the behaviors of the allies. We can garner some very helpful information for the client about how they impact the energy of the people around them. Further, we can do it in a way that continues to teach constructive feedback skills to each interviewee. Next, with all this helpful information and willing allies, is that enough for the client to make a change? There is another important ingredient described next in chapter 8.

Chapter 7 Recap

❖ The energy of the client has an impact on the allies and provides useful information to help them be versatile in their approach with each person.

❖ Social network analysis gives visual evidence of how people are connected. Within this field of study, the question "When you interact with this person, how does it affect your energy?" is highly predictive of performance.

❖ Energizing leaders impact the performance, creativity, well-being, and engagement of their team, and are higher performers themselves.

❖ Asking the energy question gives specific behavioral information to the client while also nudging the allies to further practice reframing themselves toward solutions and to notice those behaviors in real time.

Reflection Prompts:

1. Consider someone whose energy has a large effect on you. What specifically do they do that energizes you or drains you?

2. How do you feel you affect others' energy? What might be energizing or zapping to others?

3. How could you become more versatile so that your behaviors energize different people in your work or home?

CHAPTER 8

Recognizing the Importance of Motivation

Now we know what people love and appreciate about our client—their strengths as perceived by others. Moreover, we know when our client is most successful with others and what they can do to be even more effective in working with specific people—what *to do*, or solutions. We've even gone so far as to help move these stakeholders toward becoming allies in our clients' development—willing supporters who have committed to being part of our client's professional growth. We know how our client impacts the energy of others. Even more, this is being shared in a transparent and open way, bringing context to the feedback. Is that enough for change?

No.

The Development Pipeline

A common model applied to coaching is the Development Pipeline.[55] The Development Pipeline describes the conditions for change and helps coaches understand where coaching can be most beneficial. It shows behavior change as a progression through **insight**, **motivation**, **capabilities** (skills), **real-world practice**, and **accountability**.

1. Insight: Clients need to gain insight into their behaviors, perceptions, and goals. Often this is acquired through assessments, 360s, performance reviews, development conversations, etc.

2. Motivation: It is important to understand how deeply motivated the client is to achieve the desired change. How much time and energy are they willing to invest?

3. Skill: How much skill and/or knowledge is required to make the desired change? Can that skill be developed?

4. Practice: Can the client practice the new skills and create a habit to sustain those new skills?

5. Accountability: The client needs to develop accountability and reinforcement beyond the coach and the coaching engagement. This is usually with others in their "people system," so that the new skills and behaviors are reinforced after the coach is gone.

The Development Pipeline model highlights that change is constrained by the narrowest segment of the pipeline. For example, a client may have great insight into their current behavior but lack deep motivation to change. Therefore, change will be more difficult. If we apply the Development Pipeline to the Shift Positive Method, we must understand that insight (feedback on strengths and what *to do*) is necessary but not sufficient for effective change. So, we must focus on the second stage as well: gauging the client's motivation.

"Insight is necessary but not sufficient for change."

Uncovering motivation is an important step for the coach or leader and client to explore and will prove essential. It can take a lot of motivation to change because clients are often very experienced and well-practiced in the behaviors and habits they've honed. These behaviors are what have helped them to be so successful . . . so far.

Therefore, we often find that sustaining motivation is about more than just the professional realm. Themes that show up in the client's work life are often present in their personal life. We never leave ourselves at home. So, this is an opportunity to dig a little deeper. Why does the client want to change? What will sustain them?

Molly's story illustrates what we mean by deeper motivation. Molly was the head of Human Resources at a hedge fund. She was part of the executive leadership team even though she was not a partner in the firm and was at a senior director level. Molly was the only female on the leadership team and frankly the only person who was not a multimillionaire. In her feedback, she received accolades for her analytical ability, thoroughness, and attention to detail. She was unflappable. Yet, the managing partner wanted her to, "Speak up twice as much and be 80 percent accurate rather than speaking as she did already and being 100 percent accurate. We need to hear from her more—get her voice in the room."

That sounds like supportive feedback—simply wanting more engagement from Molly in the leadership team meetings. However, step back and look at the situation. Molly was the key income earner in her family, mother of two daughters, introverted, and very good at her HR role. She had a lot to risk by getting on the wrong side of the partners. So, she played it safe.

Then when the coach asked Molly about her motivation for change, she struggled to come up with an answer beyond the standard—"to make a contribution, to stretch myself, career advancement, etc." It wasn't until about a week after the 360 debrief that Molly told her coach, "I've found my motivation."

Coach: "Yes, what's that?"

Molly: "My daughter wants to quit the soccer team."

Coach: "And how does that give you your motivation?"

Molly: "Well, she's just like me. She doesn't want to try something unless she can do it well. She wants to be right, too. And, I'm the one modeling that for her. I don't want to speak up unless I'm 100 percent right."

Molly had found her motivation. It carried her through her coaching sessions. It gave her the visceral motivation she needed, in the moments during the executive leadership meetings when she felt apprehension, to speak up and put her perspective into the room. She simply had to think about her daughter.

How do we get to deeper motivation? By asking, "Suppose you've succeeded at achieving these development goals you've set for yourself—what would that mean to you?" Then, we repeatedly ask, "And what would that do for you?" "And why is that important to you?" "What would that mean to you?" We ask until the client gets to a place that is true and meaningful. It usually brings a slower pace, a deeper tone, a more adamant response, such as, "It would make a difference in the lives and families of the people on my team." "It would allow me to be home for dinner with my wife and kids and to help them with their homework." We ask until we see a change of energy or physiology in the client. Then, we're there.

Motivation of the client is critical to their sustained change. All the feedback and insight will not carry them through without tapping into deep motivation. The behaviors and habits they've honed, especially those as experienced and successful as our clients have been, are what have gotten them to their current level in the organization. However, these same behaviors and habits may need to shift in order to continue to be successful with this group of allies. So, we need to dig deeper into their motivation. Usually, it is more than professional. Themes that show up at work are often present or carry over to their personal life. If we can help the client to discover a true motivation, it can sustain them in their "next" evolution as a leader and person.

Chapter 8 Recap

❖ Insight is necessary but not sufficient for change.

❖ The development pipeline shows how the progress of change is constrained by the narrowest section of the change pipeline: Insight—Motivation—Skill—Practice—Accountability.

❖ We need to understand the client's motivation for change—a motivation that is deeply held and will sustain them while developing new behaviors and habits.

❖ Often, this motivation is more than professional; it is personal. So, digging until the client sees it and feels it is key.

Reflection Prompts:

1. Consider your own development goals. What would it mean to you to achieve these? For example, if your goal is to show up more positively in how you lead and to encourage a growth mindset among your team, what's underneath that? Why is that important? What would that do for you? Continue until you find deeper motivation. You may find it has more to do with your desire to show up positively at home with your family, and that is what truly motivates you to keep working on your developmental goal.

2. Are you clear on the motivations of those who work with or for you? What would a conversation look like where you go deeper to understand what truly matters to your staff member or teammate?

3. We manage others assuming they are motivated in the same way we are, but often that's not the case—especially across generations. What would it look like if you managed your team with their unique motivation(s) in mind?

Feedback
Reimagined

PART THREE
Exploring Possibilities

Now that you've seen how to change the feedback experience through the concepts and application of the Shift Positive Method, let's consider what else is possible.

We've been fortunate enough to bring the Shift Positive Method into several organizations through different entry points—the executive team, the HRBPs and managers, or all staff. What we have come to learn is that if you want to ensure a successful shift in mindset and culture, it matters how you introduce the model.

In the next chapter, we'll show how to successfully integrate the Shift Positive Method across every tier of an organization to create a feedback culture that thrives in psychological safety, transparency, and allyship. We'll also help you decide if this approach is right for you or your organization. Finally, in chapter 10, we'll conclude by discussing feedback moving forward and what's truly possible if we bring the Shift Positive Method into our dialogue on a regular basis.

CHAPTER 9

Building a Safe and Open Feedback Culture

Millennials are the majority generation in the workforce and have been since 2016. They are widely known for wanting continuous feedback, for wanting to be coached, not criticized. When a millennial asks for feedback, it stems from a desire to excel in their role. Contrary to how others may perceive this generation, they aren't seeking more praise. They are simply asking, "What can I do better?"

According to Stuart Hearn, CEO of Clear Review performance management platform, "You may be surprised to hear that the benefits most valued by millennial employees are training and development. Millennials, as we've established, are an ambitious bunch. The standard 9-5, 'get in and get out' attitude no longer applies. Millennials are looking for learning experiences. They want to be pushed and challenged by their employers."[56] This simply means developmental feedback is essential to culture, and how that experience is fostered is vital.

Building an effective feedback culture doesn't just happen overnight. It must be intentional and thoughtful. You have the power to create a workplace environment that meets basic human needs across generations, even when it comes to feedback. In psychologist Barry Schwartz's TED Talk, "The way we think about work is broken,"[57] he states: "The very shape of the institution within which people work creates people who are fitted to the demands of that institution, and deprives people of the opportunities to derive the kinds of satisfaction from their work that we take for granted." Essentially, this is saying that many organizations still believe we pay people to work to fulfill their most basic psychological needs of food, water, warmth, safety, and security; however, as a leader, you can do more. Schwartz concludes his TED Talk by explaining human nature will be changed by the theories we have, and he poses a challenge to all of us: What kind of human nature do you want to help design in your organization?

As we discussed in chapter 2, people need more to truly thrive. As Maggie Wooll, managing editor for BetterUp, explains, every human needs the full pyramid, especially when it comes to staying motivated. "People don't just want to fulfill their basic needs. Once people are reasonably able to meet the first four 'deficiency needs' [in Maslow's hierarchy] they can begin to focus more on their 'growth need.' Everyone has a natural desire to reach one's full potential or self-actualization."[58]

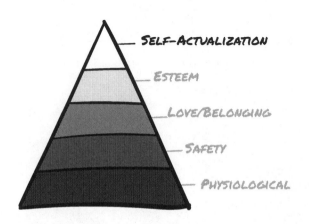

We stated in chapter 3 that to create the most impact with the Shift Positive Method, you must make your own shifts. By now, you've realized several places to shift to make feedback feel more human, energizing, and effective:

❖ A shift to a growth mindset, where you deeply believe improvement and growth are possible—a focus on effort, not labels.

❖ A shift toward seeing people with new eyes, noticing first what their strengths are and what is currently working well.

❖ A shift in both gathering feedback through solution-focused inquiry and giving feedback that identifies clear, specific desired outcomes.

❖ A shift to transparency, moving away from anonymous or confidential feedback.

❖ A shift away from one-way feedback with little to no support and instead toward creating feedback experiences grounded in two-way accountability, each person an ally in the other's growth.

❖ A shift in understanding—that feedback is relational and always relative to the person who is providing it, not factual or objective.

Each shift requires intention and application to make it stick. This starts within each of us, with our own drive and desire to shift our mindset in order to be more effective. You read earlier about the challenge of sending a changed client back to an unchanged system—that no matter how much growth and progress the client has experienced, if they go back to a system that neither recognizes nor supports their change, it will fade. So, to really change the feedback experience for all, we must create a shift across the entire organizational culture. Let's take a look at how this starts.

Language Shapes Beliefs

When we consider what drives transformational change, it helps to look beneath the surface. Often people believe that to get a different action or result out of someone, you just need to tell them to change their behavior. For example, you show someone a video of them presenting to illustrate that they use "um" as a space filler too often. In doing this, you make them aware. Occasionally, in a case like this, awareness can be self-correcting.

However, frequently a behavior is driven by a more deeply held belief. We see clients feeling "not enough" or feeling shame that impacts how they show up in the world.

For example, if a female leader believes her thoughts are undervalued because she's a woman, that can drive her thinking or self-talk that *no one cares about or listens to my point of view*, which will ultimately drive a feeling of shame, anger, or resignation—and the resulting behavior of not speaking up to voice her opinion. She might fade back or play it small. This in turn makes her feel insignificant and often reinforces the original belief: *I'm undervalued because I'm a woman.* Our beliefs drive our thoughts, and our thoughts drive our feelings and behaviors, which then drive our actions. To really create sustainable change, we need to be working at the level of a person's belief system.

Beliefs are like your operating system. Just like the code that tells the computer what to do, your beliefs essentially drive what you tell yourself, and as a result, how you choose to behave. Beliefs come from all sorts of influences, from early childhood and the beliefs of your parents to cultural and religious beliefs to your own life experiences and the beliefs you form as a result. Beliefs are also formed by the stories we tell ourselves, that critical inner dialogue that is often a form of shame.

Then, there are the beliefs within your workplace: what defines the culture, values, or the beliefs that come from your direct manager or the beliefs that trickle down from the executive team. These beliefs can vary across generations, which is especially important to understand with yet another generation entering the workforce, Gen Z. Anna Liotta, in her work *Unlocking Generational Codes*, does a brilliant job of helping us understand the beliefs of each generation based on universal shifts and world events that led to these beliefs, and how they translate into values and areas of focus. She coined the phrase "It's not personal; it's generational" to help us understand two fundamental truths: each generation believes their way of seeing the world is right and each wants respect for how they see the world.[59]

| Beliefs drive behaviors.

Successfully shifting a culture starts with shifting beliefs, and that means shifting the language that's shared across the organization. One example that's essential to the Shift Positive Method is that we don't use the word "weakness," because it can be triggering and ineffective. Instead we teach leaders to frame constructive feedback with a focus on how someone can be more effective. This promotes a growth mindset and builds the belief in the leader that change is possible. This is where the executive leadership team plays such an essential role. When working with organizations, we have seen the most impact when the top leaders truly embrace and champion this shift in mindset and beliefs. The moment you ask a question, it changes the way people think. Leaders who ask solution-focused questions to gather feedback, seek desired outcomes for how a leader could be at their very best, and focus on seeing strengths ultimately create powerful shifts.

It starts with each member of the leadership team experiencing their own shift—truly feeling for themselves how feedback can be more human and much more specific and actionable as a result. We look to create this experience by having each member of the leadership team go through the Shift Positive 360 process for themselves. We've also seen this shift occur when the entire HR team gets trained in the Shift Positive Method and brings the new language into their feedback frameworks, creating a consistent mindset on the most effective way to gather and give feedback.

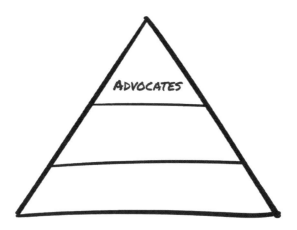

In our organizational model, we see the executive leaders of the organization, HRBPs, and talent directors as the "advocates" for these shifts. Their role is to embrace and champion the new mindset, which will in turn influence others. As they become steeped in these beliefs and a Positive Psychology mindset, it creates new language for others to adopt and embrace.

When we first engaged a leadership team at one of our largest clients in the med-device industry, we gave a keynote to get everyone grounded in the method and make sure they heard a different way of framing feedback. Then, each person was interviewed about every other team member—11 total interviews for each leader. Through this, each leader learned and practiced the shifts of looking for strengths, naming desired behaviors, offering up one thing in support, and gaining comfort in knowing all of the feedback is fully transparent. Each time we brought them together, we reminded them of the framework for how to give feedback in a safe and human way—leading with what you appreciate about someone's strengths, expressing how they could be even more effective, and offering support toward their development. This is now common language among the team, and the president commented, "I've never seen this before. It's embarrassing for the world that this is the first we've seen an approach like this. The Shift Positive Method is profound!"

Awareness and Application Support New Behaviors

While a new belief will ultimately drive a different behavior, it will take practice for that behavior to become habit. While it's powerful to learn something new and understand how it's different and why it's effective, it's even more powerful to learn how to apply it yourself.

With this book, we set out with the goal to make you aware of how we are wired as humans and how that makes feedback challenging. In understanding why feedback is hard, you can better appreciate why we have designed the Shift Positive Method as it is. Your understanding goes even further when you experience this type of feedback yourself, allowing you to feel your own shifts, insights, and impact—to shift your beliefs. Then you can apply it to your own day-to-day dialogue. With new beliefs, you'll exhibit new behaviors and new ways of being. When you experience strengths-focused feedback and have countless examples from your colleagues describing you at your absolute best, it shifts how you see yourself. It also builds your own belief in the importance of strengths-based feedback. In turn, you'll show up differently when giving others feedback; you'll be more inclined to see and communicate the strengths you see in others.

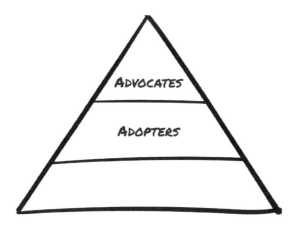

The managers and leaders who are responsible for giving feedback every day are the group that benefits the most in experiencing their own shifts and then understanding how to apply these new ways of being. It is essential that they not only grasp this new mindset and approach but also actively learn how to use it through interactive application and practice, allowing them to model the method effectively with others. We call this group the "adopters." We learned in coach training at the Hudson Institute that adults learn best when they are taught a concept, then given a chance to apply it and make it relevant to themselves and their situation to help it to stick. We take a similar approach with our clients by introducing the Shift Positive concepts, followed by letting each person experience feedback themselves so they feel the power of these concepts. We take it a step further as they then apply the concepts to their teams, learning how to give feedback in the Shift Positive way.

One of the ways we've made the Shift Positive Method more scalable for organizations and large groups of leaders is by creating an alternative to the full 360 narrative interview approach. For each manager, we conduct a live, facilitated session with their direct reports and focus on three core areas: strengths, growth, and allyship; this method is called the Shift Positive Live. While it does not provide the full system view that the Shift Positive 360 does, the Shift Positive Live still includes the most essential areas for a leader to focus on to create a strong development plan.

One of our Fortune 50 tech clients created a DEI leadership development program to accelerate the careers of a diverse group of high potentials, 24 in total, in 2021. The desired outcomes were that each leader would feel valued by the company, grow as a leader and as a person, and have a more defined career path as a result. For the company, this would bring more diverse leaders in through the development pipeline. The core components of the proposed program included: feedback and a development plan, monthly sessions with an external coach, an internal executive sponsor, and a team project to complete. The company wanted to offer a feedback component that would be effective yet different from the existing internal feedback systems.

We recommended a Shift Positive Live for each of the leaders, which would include a live, facilitated feedback session with six of their self-selected peers, their direct reports, and their sponsor, conducted by a certified Shift Positive Live coach. This approach allowed the Shift Positive Method to be scaled to a group of 24 and kick off the entire program. Each leader had a kickoff call to meet their coach and do their own "self-assessment," focusing on the same three desired outcomes. Next, the Shift Positive coach spent 75 minutes on Zoom with six colleagues of the leader, collecting feedback on the leader's strengths and growth, as well as garnering commitments of support. Immediately following the Live session, the leader and coach then debriefed the results with full transparency about who said what, as well as each ally's commitment of support. Next, the leader distilled the feedback into a development plan with up to three focus areas of growth, the strengths to leverage, and a list of each ally and how they would support the leader. Each leader then began monthly sessions with their coach for the remainder of the program (six months).

Within three months following the program, of the 24 DEI participants, 44 percent were promoted. And 93 percent agreed or strongly agreed that the program made a significant impact on their leadership development. The Shift Positive Live feedback portion of the program was rated as the most impactful. When participants were asked to rate their response to the statement *The Shift Positive experience has enhanced my leadership growth*, Shift Positive Live rated 6.48 on a 7-point scale. Participant comments ranged from "Shift Positive review and feedback was phenomenal, and immediately gave me stuff that I could action right away" to "The feedback from the Shift Positive session— I loved every moment of it. I wasn't sure what to expect, but it was my favorite part by far. It has helped me with my relationships. Even though I had really good relationships, it helped even more."

The program has now been recommended as a future annual program for high potentials. The organization has also recreated their new leader assimilation process to fall in line with the Shift Positive Method.

"I'll say most impactful, for sure, was the Shift Positive Live session."

What's great about rolling out the Shift Positive Method across the organization is that the more leaders experience feedback in the Shift Positive way, the more they use the concepts themselves with others. For stakeholders, just by participating in giving feedback to another through the Shift Positive Method, they begin to shift themselves. Even more, they will become empowered to request feedback for themselves in a more effective way.

Given the amount of feedback managers are now expected to give (Gen Z is asking for it several times a month), well beyond an annual or semi-annual performance review, companies need to ensure they are arming managers with the tools and training to do this well. While we hope this book will do much of that for you, we also have a manager training called Shift Positive Applied specifically for those front-line leaders who find themselves in weekly one-on-ones with ample opportunity to give developmental feedback. In a similar applied learning approach, this training offers a deeper dive into the concepts with interactive exercises to practice and debrief among cross-functional colleagues.

We worked with one advertising agency that, after having a few of their leadership team receive a Shift Positive 360, asked us to train up all their leaders with direct reports. Every employee had already taken the Gallup CliftonStrengths (even new employees took it on their first day), so we were able to naturally build on their strengths data while also incorporating the T-chart method, Appreciative Inquiry, and building allyship. Each leader brought real-time situations to help craft effective feedback for several members of their team. The training didn't just lead to new language and reframing of existing feedback questions; it also created more thoughtful and in-depth conversations that reached well beyond the initial annual review conversations they were preparing for. One participant shared, "This training really helped to reframe and reforecast a way forward for myself and my team. From the very first video, Jen stopped me in my tracks and engaged me in the next day of training. Hurrah for such a thoughtful and enlightened platform that has allowed me to build the coming year for our people and clients." The application of the concepts is what clarified the difference of approach and ultimately gave the leaders a safe place to practice and refine their most effective feedback conversations.

Empowered Ambassadors Shift the Culture

Millennials are predicted to comprise 75 percent of the global workforce in 2025. When we consider what it will take to truly create a cultural shift in feedback, ensuring that the approach resonates with the masses will be critical to ensuring it sticks. As we've discussed, millennials are highly motivated to succeed; they have high expectations of their managers to help create that path while coaching them to reach their full potential along the way. Imagine if Millenials and all of today's workforce were empowered to seek out their own effective feedback while building personalized systems of support to help ensure their success.

This can be done by leveraging existing technology platforms within companies (HRIS systems, Slack, performance management systems, etc.) and, with small modifications, making them consistent with and leverage the Shift Positive Method.

We see a future of organizations that are promoting a Shift Positive mindset—starting at the executive level, across the HR functions, and through each and every manager and individual contributor. This creates a culture of "ambassadors" where anyone at any level is empowered to request their own developmental feedback through the Shift Positive Method. People feel safe doing so because they trust the mindset shifts that have occurred across the organization.

Imagine you are one of these ambassadors at your organization and you're empowered to request your own developmental feedback. You know your colleagues will be looking for what is working and naming your specific strengths—looking for and naming examples of you at your best. You also trust that any feedback giver will go beyond a problem or weakness-focus and frame the constructive feedback through the lens of a solution, naming the desired behaviors for you to practice to become more effective. And, finally, each person providing feedback is open, transparent, and willing to remain a part of the process by offering up one specific way to support your growth, knowing that we simply do not change alone. As a result, you're genuinely excited to receive this feedback, and it feels much more psychologically safe to solicit. This changes the feedback experience for all.

> Each person is invested in the individual and collective paths toward thriving.

This goes beyond a culture about feedback; it builds a culture centered around growth and development, where each person is invested in the individual and collective paths toward thriving. Considering the ties between feedback and retention, the Shift Positive Method creates a safe and energizing feedback experience centered on growth, development, and support, paving the way for today's workforce.

Knowing if Your Organization Is Ready

Creating shifts at an individual level or organizational level can be simple by definition, but that does not mean it's easy. We say that to our clients all the time. As we've stated, this takes intention and commitment from each level of the organization, beginning with the executive leadership. It requires a willingness to detach from the way we've been conditioned to think—the belief that we need the hard, critical feedback and that we must focus on fixing our weaknesses, or that feedback should be anonymous or confidential. This may be too far of a reach for a culture that has been operating this way for decades. We get it. We're suggesting something counter to well-worn beliefs and even against our own biology (remember Negativity Bias and the SCARF model from chapter 2). However, what is the impact of no change at all? Of continuing to use feedback systems that are counter to how we grow and thrive?

Considering the cost of engagement, retention, and employee development, the impact seems quite high. Combined with the high expectations of today's workforce, the impact of no change may be too severe. That said, even if you are not sure you're fully "ready" to embrace a new way of thinking and new behaviors around feedback, we ask: *Are you open?* Are you open to seeing development through new eyes? Are you open to asking different questions? Are you open to being more transparent in feedback? Are you open to being accountable for the feedback you provide to others, being an active participant in their development? Are you open to building a culture of constructive feedback? If this is you, and you believe your executive team will bring the same level of openness, then that's step one—a place to start reimagining the feedback culture at your organization.

Chapter 9 Recap:

❖ Millennials will continue to make up the majority of the workforce, and they, along with Gen Z, demand frequent developmental feedback.

❖ Every human craves an opportunity to reach their full potential, and it's up to each organization to decide how to create a human experience for all to grow and thrive.

❖ Language shapes beliefs, and it's up to a company's executive leadership team, HRBPs, and change agents to be the "advocates" of this shift in mindset for the entire organization.

❖ Awareness and application allow new behaviors to become new ways of being; it's essential that all managers within the company become the "adopters" of the method, both by experiencing the shift and by learning how to model it in their day-to-day feedback conversations.

❖ Leveraging "ambassadors" around the company is what will ultimately create a culture shift. With a new unified mindset for growth and development, all levels are empowered to gather their own feedback through the Shift Positive Method.

❖ While it's not easy to drive change, if you and your organization are truly open to seeing people, and feedback, through new eyes—that's step one.

Reflection Prompts:

1. What would it look like if you provided feedback more often? What's one thing you could do differently when gathering or giving feedback to support what you've learned here?

2. Where can you make some simple shifts in your own beliefs to drive more effective behaviors and help you to achieve your goals?

3. What are one or two small steps you could take to help your organization build a more constructive feedback culture?

CHAPTER 10

Feedback Moving Forward

Feedback is hard—it *feels* hard. We've detailed why: our biology and psychology (negativity bias, SCARF, mindset) all impact how we give and receive feedback. The way behaviors are noticed and feedback is delivered is in direct contrast to how we're wired to receive it. We need to feel psychological safety. Further, the feedback systems today are largely broken from a design and delivery perspective. When research shows that feedback is causing more harm than good in many cases, it's time for a significant change. We hope by now you've come to see why it's so important that feedback evolve to the needs of today's workforce that feedback becomes more human, and as a result, more effective.

As a society and across organizations, we're seeing the importance of creating cultures that are psychologically safe. In order to improve the feedback experience, we start by evolving it to feel safe—building trust that the intention of the feedback is truly supportive. This takes intention and some very specific components. Things such as transparency—saying no to anonymous feedback. A focus on a person's strengths—the impact they drive and ways they can leverage their strengths even further. A shift from problem-focused feedback or weakness to more solution-focused, desired behaviors—naming what *to do* is more actionable and less likely to be triggering. Offering feedback in an ongoing, timely manner, especially catching people doing things well. And finally, a willingness from anyone who's giving the feedback (manager to employee, peer to peer, etc.) to take an active part in the growth and development journey by offering specific support for any feedback that's given while being an ally actively looking for and reinforcing the positive change.

We believe that through research, application, and continued experimentation and refinement, we have crafted a method that addresses this dire need to change the feedback experience for today's workforce—the Shift Positive Method. Our goal was to leverage the field of Positive Psychology and make it applicable and actionable to the redesign of feedback. Further, we have illustrated how to shift feedback away from one-way dialogue and into a two-way accountability by creating an entire system of support within the feedback experience. Effective feedback should create connection between people—by asking for feedback and thoughtfully giving feedback in an open, transparent way.

As we look ahead and consider the future for feedback, we see a world where the Shift Positive Method can have impact for anyone, in any relationship. One of our favorite memories from a coach certification training occurred years ago, when we role-played the T-chart method. We asked for a volunteer to be live-coached through their T-chart, articulating the shift from problem-focused to more solution-focused. A masterful coach raised his hand and said he had done his T-chart exercise on his five-year-old son. So, we asked him to go ahead and name what was on the left side: What are some of the things he'd like to see change?

He shared that his son was five and daughter was three, and he wanted to see his son be nicer to his daughter. He wanted his son to stop being mean to her and excluding her from play. He said, "He's not a great big brother to her." Okay, so we felt clear enough on the left side issues, so we moved to the right side. We said: "How could your son be a better big brother?" "What would 'nice' look like?" You could see John thinking it through, almost as if it was the $64 million question. We probed more: "What would it look like if he was behaving like a good big brother—what would he be doing?" He talked it through a bit, and then he finally said with clarity, "He'd share his toys with her like he shares his camera with the neighbor boy." There it was—clarity, action, and something to start doing (versus stop doing). We asked: "Do you think your son will understand if you give him this feedback?" He said, "Yes, absolutely—thank you!"

For nearly the last decade, we have used this method over and over with leaders and organizations with great success. We have watched the lightbulbs go off for each leader as they (for the first time, in many cases) received clear, actionable feedback that also left them feeling seen, energized, and motivated. As a result, we've seen far more successful shifts and development emerge as leaders work their plans, staying focused on strengths, growth, and leveraging their allies. This, in turn, energized us to share this method with readers like you around the globe, so together, we can reimagine what's possible.

We close by inviting you to reimagine a world where you communicate differently, starting with your willingness to see people through new eyes. To notice people for their strengths. To deeply believe that with practice and support, we can improve, grow, and change. A world where you offer solution-focused feedback, naming desired behaviors instead of weaknesses to help others be their most effective. Where there is psychological safety that allows you to be fully transparent. And finally, a place where you can always look to your left and to your right and see an ally—someone truly invested in helping you to thrive. Now, this feels like the gift feedback was always intended to be, and we invite you to join us in creating a more energized and connected world, one relationship at a time.

Endnotes

1   Hearn, S. n.d. "5 Reasons Why Millennials Crave Ongoing Feedback." Recruiter.com. https://www.recruiter.com/i/5-reasons-why-millennials-crave-ongoing-feedback/.

2   Willyerd, K. February 27, 2015. "Millennials Want to Be Coached at Work." *Harvard Business Review*. https://hbr.org/2015/02/millennials-want-to-be-coached-at-work?registration=success.

3   Yoon, J., Blunden, H., Kristal, A., Whillans, A. September 20, 2019. "Why Asking for Advice is More Effective than Asking for Feedback." *Harvard Business Review*. https://hbr.org/2019/09/why-asking-for-advice-is-more-effective-than-asking-for-feedback.

4   Rock, D. 2008. "SCARF: a brain-based model for collaborating with and influencing others." *NeuroLeadership Journal* 1 (1): 1–9.

5   Rock, D. 2009. "Managing with the brain in mind." *Strategy + Business* 56.

6   Eisenberger, N. and Lieberman, M. 2009. "The pains and pleasures of social life: Explication of social pain and social pleasure, and the impact of fairness, status, and autonomy on brain response." *Science* 323 (5916): 890–891.

7   Eisenberger, N., Lieberman, M., and Williams, K. D. 2003. "Does rejection hurt? An fMRI study of social exclusion," *Science* 302 (5643): 290–292.

8   Berinato, S. 2018. "Negative Feedback Rarely Leads to Improvement." *Harvard Business Review* 96 (1): 32–33.

9   Dweck, C. S. 2002. "Messages that motivate: How praise molds students' beliefs, motivation, and performance (in surprising ways)." In *Improving academic achievement:*

Impact of psychological factors on education, edited by J. Aronson, 37–60. Academic Press. https://doi.org/10.1016 /B978-012064455-1/50006-3.

10 Wilkie, D. 2015. "Is the annual performance review dead?" SHRM. https://www.shrm.org/resourcesandtools/hr -topics/employee-relations/pages/performance-reviews-are -dead.aspx.

11 Nowack, K. M., and Mashihi, S. 2012. "Evidence-based answers to 15 questions about leveraging 360-degree feedback." *Consulting Psychology Journal: Practice and Research* 64 (3): 157–182.

12 Kluger, A. N., and DeNisi, A. 1996. "The effects of feedback interventions on performance: A historical review, a meta-analysis, and a preliminary feedback theory." *Psychological Bulletin* 119: 254–284.

13 Rath, T. 2007. *StrengthsFinder 2.0*. Gallup Press.

14 Google ReWork. n.d. *Understand team effectiveness.* https://rework.withgoogle.com/print/guides /5721312655835136/.

15 Edmondson, A. C., and Lei, Z. 2014. "Psychological safety: The history, renaissance, and future of an inter-personal construct." *Annual Review of Organizational Psychology and Organizational Behavior* 1: 23–43. https:// doi.org/10.1146/annurev-orgpsych-031413-091305.

16 Coutifaris, C., and Grant, A. M. 2021. "Taking Your Team Behind the Curtain: The Effects of Leader Feedback-Sharing and Feedback-Seeking on Team Psychological Safety." *Organization Science.* https://doi.org/10.1287 /orsc.2021.1498.

17 Mayer, R. C., Davis, J. H., and Schoorman, F. D. 1995. "An integrative model of organizational trust." *The Academy of Management Review* 20 (3): 709–734. https://doi.org /10.2307/258792.

18 Buckingham, M., and Goodall, A. 2019. "The Feedback Fallacy." *Harvard Business Review.*

19 Dorsey, J. and Villa, D. 2018. *The State of Gen Z 2018.* https://genhq.com/generation-z-research-2018/.

20 Buckingham, M. 2007. *Strengths-based Thinking & Application.* [Video] YouTube. https://www.youtube.com /watch?v=4lNC6--JuoY&t=3s.

21 Fredrickson, B. 2001. "The role of positive emotions in Positive Psychology: The Broaden-&-Build Theory of positive emotions." *American Psychologist* 36 (3): 218–226.

22 Fredrickson, B. September 11, 2010. "Understanding positive emotions." [Class] University of Pennsylvania, MAPP 600: Introduction to Positive Psychology. Philadelphia.

23 Fisher, C. D. 2000. "Mood and emotions while working: missing pieces of job satisfaction?" *Journal of Organizational Behavior* 21: 185–202.

24 Achor, S. 2013. *Before happiness: The 5 hidden keys to achieving success, spreading happiness, and sustaining positive change.* New York: Crown Business.

25 Dweck, C. S. 2002. "Messages that Motivate." *Improving Academic Achievement*, Elsevier.

26 Bronson, P. 2007. "How Not to Talk to Your Kids." *New York Magazine.* http://nymag.com/news/features/27840/.

27 Senge, P. M. 1990. *The Fifth Discipline: The Art & Practice of the Learning Organization.* New York: Doubleday.

28 Goldsmith, M. and Morgan, H. 2004. "Leadership is a contact sport: The follow-up factor in management development." *Strategy + Business* 36: 71–79.

29 Buckingham, M. January 29, 2020. *Defining Strengths.* [Video] https://www.marcusbuckingham.com/defining -strengths/.

30 CliftonStrengths. n.d. "What is the difference between a talent and strength?" https://hope.gallup.com/help/general/273908/difference-talent-strength.aspx.

31 Seligman, M. E., Steen, T. A., Park, N., and Peterson, C. 2005. "Positive Psychology progress: Empirical validation of interventions." *American Psychologist* 60 (5): 410–421. doi:https://psycnet.apa.org/doiLanding?doi=10.1037%2F0003-066X.60.5.410.

32 Rath, T. 2007. *StrengthsFinder 2.0*. Gallup Press.

33 Glassdoor. November 13, 2013. "More than half of employees would stay longer at their company if bosses showed more appreciation, glassdoor survey." https://www.glassdoor.com/about-us/employees-stay-longer-company-bosses-showed-appreciation-glassdoor-survey/.

34 Biswas-Diener, R. 2010. *Practicing Positive Psychology Coaching: Assessment, Activities, and Strategies for Success*. Hoboken, NJ: John Wiley & Sons, Inc.

35 Fritz, C. and Taylor, Morgan R. 2022. "Taking in the good: How to facilitate savoring in work organizations." *Business Horizons* 65: 139–148.

36 Bryant, F. B. 2003. "Savoring beliefs inventory (SBI): A scale for measuring beliefs about savouring." *Journal of Mental Health* 12 (2): 175–196.

37 Biswas-Diener, R., Kashdan, T.B., and Lyubchik, N. 2016. "Psychological strengths at work." *The Wiley Blackwell Handbook of the Psychology of Positivity and Strengths-Based Approaches at Work*. Eds. Oades, L. G., Steger, M. F., Fave, A. D., and Passmore, J.). https://doi.org/10.1002/9781118977620.ch3.

38 Fredrickson, B. 2001. "The role of positive emotions in Positive Psychology." *American Psychologist*.

39 Szabo, P., Meier, D., and Dierolf, K. 2009. *Coaching, plain & simple: Solution-focused brief coaching essentials*. New York: W. W. Norton & Company.

40 Grant, A. 2012. "Making positive change: A randomized study comparing solution-focused vs. problem-focused coaching questions." *Journal of Systemic Therapies* 31 (2): 21–35.

41 Sternin, J. "The Viet Nam Story" Narrated by Jerry Sternin. https://docplayer.net/21120610-The-viet-nam -story-narrarted-by-jerry-sternin.html.

42 Cooperrider, D. L., Whitney D. K., and Stavros, J. M. 2008. *Appreciative Inquiry Handbook for Leaders of Change.* 2nd ed. Brunswick, OH: Crown Custom Publishing, Inc.

43 Bushe, G. R., and Kassam, A. F. 2005. "When is Appreciative Inquiry transformational? A meta-case analysis." *Journal of Applied Behavioral Science* 41 (2): 161–181.

44 Buckingham, M., and Goodall, A. 2019. "The Feedback Fallacy." *Harvard Business Review.*

45 Schnall, S., Harber, K. D., Stefanucci, J. K., and Proffitt, D. R. 2008. "Social support and the perception of geographical slant." *Journal of Experimental Social Psychology* 44: 1246–1255.

46 Thoits, P. A. 1986. "Social support as coping assistance." *Journal of Consulting and Clinical Psychology* 54: 416–423.

47 Cohen, S., Doyle, W. J., Turner, R., Alper, C. M., and Skoner, D. P. 2003. "Sociability and susceptibility to the common cold." *Psychological Science* 14, 389–395.

48 Seeman, T. E., and Syme, S. L. 1987. "Social networks and coronary artery disease: A comparison of the structure and function of social relations as predictors of disease." *Psychosomatic Medicine* 49: 341–354.

49 Fawzy, F. I., Fawzy, N. W., Hyun, C. S., Elashoff, R., Guthrie, D., Fahley, J. L., et al. 1993. "Malignant melanoma: Effects of an early structures psychiatric intervention, coping, and affective state on recurrence and

survival 6 years later." *Archives of General Psychiatry* 50: 681–689.

50 Baker, W., Cross, R., and Wooten, M. 2003. "Positive organizational network analysis and energizing relationships." In *Positive Organizational Scholarship: Foundations of a New Discipline*, by K. Cameron, J. Dutton and R. Quinn, 328–342. Oakland, CA: Berrett-Koehler Publishers.

51 Cross, R., Linder, J. C., Parker, A. 2008. "Charged up: Managing the energy that drives innovation. The network roundtable at the university of Virginia." [Report] https:// kipdf.com/charged-up-managing-the-energy-that-drives -innovation_5ac1935f1723ddf5cb10ebb7.html.

52 Owens, B., Baker, W., and Cameron, K. S. 2013. "Relational Energy at Work: Establishing Construct, Nomological, and Predictive Validity." Working paper. Center for Positive Organizational Scholarship, University of Michigan.

53 Baker W. 2001. *Achieving Success Through Social Capital*. San Francisco: Josey-Bass.

54 Spreitzer, G. M., Lam, C. F., and Quinn, R. W. 2012. "Human Energy in Organizations." In *Oxford Handbook of Positive Organizational Scholarship*, eds. Cameron, K. S., Spreitzer, G. M., 155–67. New York: Oxford University Press.

55 Peterson, D. B. 2006. "People are complex and the world is messy: A behavior-based approach to executive coaching." In *Evidence Based Coaching Handbook: Putting Best Practices to Work for Your Clients*, eds. Stober, D., and Grant, A, 51–76. Hoboken, NJ: John Wiley & Sons.

56 Hearn, S. n.d. "5 Reasons Why Millennials Crave Ongoing Feedback." Recruiter.com.

57 Schwartz, B. March 2014. "The way we think about work is broken." [Video] TED 2014 Talk. Vancouver, BC.

https://www.ted.com/talks/barry_schwartz_the_way_we
_think_about_work_is_broken?language=en.

58 Wooll, M. December 3, 2021. "Watch your language! (it
shapes company culture)." BetterUp. https://www.betterup
.com/blog/company-language#:~:text=Although%20
we%20may%20not%20realize,and%20feel%20in%20
different%20situations.

59 Liotta, A. 2012. *Unlocking Generational Codes*. New York:
Aviva Publishing.

Appendix

T-Chart Method	
Problem-Focused	Solution-Focused

Additional Resources

Appreciative Inquiry by David Cooperrider, PhD
(Berrett-Koehler Publishers, 2005)

The Art of Possibility by Benjamin Zander
(Penguin Books, 2002)

Coaching Plain & Simple by Peter Szabo & Daniel Meier
(W. W. Norton & Company, 2009)

Flourish by Martin Seligman, PhD (Atria, 2012)

The Happiness Advantage and *Before Happiness*
by Shawn Achor, MA (Crown Publishing Group, 2010, 2013)

Mindset by Carol Dweck, PhD (Ballantine Books, 2007)

1,001 Solution-Focused Questions by Fredrike Bannink, MDR
(W. W. Norton & Company, 2010)

Positivity by Barbara Fredrickson, PhD (Harmony, 2009)

Practicing Positive Leadership by Kim Cameron, PhD
(Berrett-Koehler Publishers, 2013)

Practicing Positive Psychology Coaching
by Robert Biswas-Diener, MS (Wiley, 2010)

Unlocking Generational Codes by Anna Liotta
(Aviva Publishing, 2012)

Your Brain at Work by David Rock, PhD
(Harper Business, 2020)

Gallup CliftonStrengths: www.gallup.com – An online strengths assessment to learn about your top five strengths.

Values in Action Character Strengths: www.viacharacter.org – An online strengths assessment to learn about your character strengths.

Acknowledgments

Jenny Peterson, you got this all started by saying, "I hear your interviews and the impact they have. You really have something here. What will it take to make it go?" With that, Pete and Jen connected again and launched Change Positive and the Shift Positive 360. You've been there with love and support every step of the way as we pursue this mission.

Thank you to the MAPP community for your positive response to an Ignite talk in 2014 that encouraged us to take this method forward (and for the many who have since become certified). To our Hudson community of coaches who have become certified and continue to encourage us. To the faculty and students of the University of St. Thomas Executive Coach Certificate program (now Center for Coaching in Organizations) for your support and for expanding the reach of this method by becoming certified coaches, thank you.

To our Shift Positive Community of coaches and HR/L&D/OD professionals who've gone through the certification and regularly offer support and refinement and share so generously with us and each other. A special thank you to our Shift Partners who expand our organization whenever needed to bring your tremendous coaching skills to bear for client engagements.

To the internal leaders and OD professionals who believed in us and Shift Positive enough to bring it into your organizations, we thank you. To name a few: Brian Shea, Lindsey Bauer, Scott

Holstine, Jessica Amortegui, Kenneth Smith, Victoria Sevilla, Brad Austin, Rob Sloyan, Ty Silberhorn, Troy Johnson, Marci Rogers, Keesha Jean-Baptiste, Leah Heck, Diane Butler, Katie Overland, and Lila Rutten.

To the countless leaders who were open enough to experience a new approach to feedback through our 360 or Live sessions, and who participated in our training sessions—we wouldn't be here if it wasn't for you. We do what we do for you.

To Jamie Shapiro, we so appreciate your vision, grace, and strength of character. You saw a bigger vision for Shift Positive and pressed us to build a technology platform after you experienced it and brought it to your clients. Your faith, investment, connections, challenge for us to write this book, and love and friendship mean the world to us.

To our Positive Psychology teachers and researchers—Marty Seligman, Shawn Achor, Ed Diener, Robert Biswas-Diener, David Cooperrider, Kim Cameron, Adam Grant, Angela Duckworth, Barbara Fredrickson, Carol Dweck, Marcus Buckingham, Chris Peterson, Jonathan Haidt, and more— thank you for flipping that switch and challenging us to look for what makes life worth living, studying it, applying it, and trying to make the world just a little brighter.

To our many friends and supporters: Nick White, the Holy Molys, the MasterMind Group, the Herons, Mary Jo Greil, Linda Newlin, Kris and Rand Harrington, and so many others—we appreciate you.

To Jake Ostrich and Shawn Ostrich, every single step of the way you've had my back and encouraged me along this journey with Pete. Thank you!

To Catherine Gregory and Nathan Joblin of Modern Wisdom Press, thank you for shepherding us through this process with so much expertise and grace.

And to my co-author, Jen, we did it! I'm forever grateful to you for joining with me and seeing the potential; for always saying, "This is so much more than a 360!" and for putting your heart into it for the last six-plus years.

To my co-author, Pete, the best "Hell YES" I ever said was in October of 2015 when you asked if I would partner with you to bring this approach into the world. Look at us now! Thank you for modeling grace, generosity, and partnership in a way that's made me a better human. Thank you for being my teacher of Positive Psychology. And thank you for listening to and laughing at my standup comedy sets.

About the Authors

Pete Berridge, MAPP, PCC,
Co-founder, CEO, Change Positive, LLC

Peter Berridge is an accomplished coach and facilitator who utilizes the sciences of Positive Psychology and executive coaching to help individuals, teams, and organizations be more engaged, effective, and productive. Pete became a certified coach through the Hudson Institute of Santa Barbara and is adjunct faculty with the Center for Coaching Organizations. He is one of the first 200 people in the world with a Master of Applied Positive Psychology (MAPP) degree from the University of Pennsylvania, the study of human strengths and well-being, and employs proven methods to promote the flourishing of people, organizations, and communities. It is with this training that the Shift Positive 360 was born. Pete was determined to bring the benefits of Positive Psychology into the feedback process, which led him to co-create Change Positive, LLC. Pete has 25+ years of coaching (more than 5,000 hours of individual coaching), facilitation, and Human Resources leadership experience. Pete's passion is coaching senior executives, rising leaders, teams, and organizations that are navigating challenges and charting new directions. When he's not exercising his passion for coaching, he's either whittling a bird out of wood or enjoying the sunset over a Minnesota lake with his Labrador, Lloyd, and incredible wife, Jenny.

Jen Ostrich, PCC, CEO, Grow Collective

Jen is a skillful executive coach, facilitator, speaker, and now author. As the CEO of the Grow Collective, she leads the charge in coaching, creating, and facilitating content that empowers leaders and teams. Her grow-effect model leverages both psychology and neuroscience to unlock one's ability to grow to thrive. Through intuitive brain-based coaching, strategic thinking, and authentic communication, Jen brings a unique ability to think like a coach, a business, and a brand. Jen began coaching on her own in 2012 when she launched ostrich coaching + consulting, focused on developing creative leaders in the advertising industry (after a 14-year career in the business). In 2016, she co-created and launched the Shift Positive Method, a revolutionary approach to feedback grounded in Positive Psychology + Allyship, making it highly effective. In 2021, Jen was named one of the Top 20 Coaches in Austin, Texas, by *Influence Digest*. Jen was trained at the prestigious Hudson Institute in 2011 and today is a PCC level coach through the ICF. Since 2017 she's been an active certified practitioner and huge believer in the Integrative9 Enneagram. Additionally, she is a graduate of the School of Communications at the Pennsylvania State University with a BA in Advertising/PR and a minor in Business. In her free time, she can be found at a 5:30 a.m. CrossFit class or eating her way through Austin with her outrageously handsome Vizsla/Lab mix, Koko.

Index

Thank You

Dear Reader, we hope our book has been informative and insightful and has inspired a positive shift in thinking about your approach to feedback. We also have a special gift just for you. Go to https://shiftpositive360.com/feedbackreimagined/gift to download a T-chart fillable pdf with video instruction on moving from problem-focused to solution-focused feedback.

We invite you to reach out and connect—we'd love to discuss how the Shift Positive Method can help you.

Learn more about our offerings for coaches
and organizations at
www.shiftpositive360.com

Made in the USA
Columbia, SC
21 March 2023

14092397R00124